Legends and Lore of the Lowcountry

A Collection of Trivia and Stories about Charleston, SC

Karen Lee

Copyright © 2023 Karen Lee

All rights reserved.

No portion of this book may be reproduced in any form without written permission from the publisher or author, except as permitted by U.S. copyright law.

ISBN: 9798852074669

DEDICATION

This book is dedicated to the rich tapestry of history, culture, natural beauty, and stories that define the Lowcountry of South Carolina. From the picturesque landscapes and charming towns to the amazing people who call this place home, it has left an indelible mark on the hearts and minds of those who have ventured into your embrace.

CONTENTS

Introduction 10

Chapter 1: Discovering the Lowcountry 12

    How Did the Lowcountry Get Its Name? 12

    When Was the Lowcountry Settled? 12

    Geography 13

    Lowcountry Counties 15

    Lowcountry Cities & Towns 16

    Major Roads and Highways 17

    Rivers and Waterways 19

    Charleston Harbor 20

    Why do People Visit? 22

    Famous Landmarks of the Lowcountry 23

    Why Is the Lowcountry Important? 25

Chapter 2: Roots and Resilience: The Rich History and Vibrant Culture of the Lowcountry 28

    A Short History 28

    Lowcountry Culture 29

    The People 31

    Historic Moments 33

    The Lowcountry and the US Military 34

    Military Monuments 35

    More Lowcountry History 37

    Lowcountry Inventions 38

Chapter 3 Preserving the Past: Museums of the Lowcountry 41

The Charleston Museum..41

The Gibbes Museum of Art..42

Charleston Museum Homes..43

The International African American Museum....................................44

Maritime and Military Museums..45

Natural History Museums...46

Chapter 4 Famous People of the Lowcounty 49

Historical Figures 49

Actors and Actresses 51

Musicians..52

Writers 53

Politicians 55

Athletes 57

Chapter 5 Haunted History: Supernatural Tales from the Lowcountry
....59

Haunted Places 59

The Ghost of Emily Geiger 62

The Ghost of Anne Bonny..63

The Gray Man of Isle of Palms 64

The Ghost of Alice Flagg 65

The Haunting of Lands End Road..66

Famous Lowcountry Cemeteries 67

Animal Spirits 69

Chapter 6 Lowcountry Cuisine: A Taste of Southern Tradition 71

Traditional Dishes 71

Seafood 72

Beverages 73

Sweet Tea 74

Sweets and Treats 75

The Oldest Restaurants & Bars 79

The Oldest Liquor Store in the United States 80

Chapter 7: The Natural Treasures of the Lowcountry: A Journey Through Its Landscapes and Wildlife 81

Outdoor Activities 82

Beaches 83

Kayaking & Paddleboarding 84

Biking 86

Wildlife 88

The Angel Oak 89

The Southeastern Wildlife Exposition 90

Conservation 91

Chapter 8 Sports and Recreation 93

Boating 93

Fishing 95

Fishing Tournaments 96

Golf 97

Tennis 99

Amateur Sports 100

Hilton Head Island Concours d'Elegance 101

The Cooper River Bridge Run 102

Chapter 9 Lowcountry Arts and Entertainment: From Gullah Traditions to World-Class Performances 104

    Spoleto Festival USA 104

    Charleston Wine + Food Festival 105

    Charleston Fashion Week 106

    Charleston Jazz Festival 107

    The High Water Festival 107

    The Charleston Bluegrass Festival 108

    The Lowcountry Cajun Festival 109

    Southern Ground Music and Food Festival 109

    Sweetgrass Cultural Arts Festival 110

    Gullah/Geechee Nation International Music & Movement Festival 111

Conclusion 113

INTRODUCTION

Welcome to "Legends and Lore of the Lowcountry: A Collection of Trivia and Stories". This book celebrates the rich culture, history, and folklore of South Carolina's Lowcountry. The region is known for its unique blend of African American heritage, Gullah Geechee culture, and Southern charm. From haunted places and ghostly legends to famous figures and mouth-watering cuisine, the Lowcountry is a treasure trove of stories and trivia that capture the spirit of this beloved region.

In this book, we will explore the fascinating stories and little-known facts that make the Lowcountry so special. You will discover the heroic tales of Emily Geiger and the Gray Man, as well as the tragic story of Alice Flagg. You'll learn about the famous figures who hail from the Lowcountry, from actors and musicians to authors and politicians. You'll also discover the region's unique cuisine, featuring traditional dishes like shrimp and grits and she-crab soup.

Beyond the history and culture, the Lowcountry is also a place of natural beauty and wonder. You'll explore the region's wildlife, from dolphins and sea turtles to alligators and birds. You'll also discover the iconic landmarks and attractions, from historic homes and museums to beaches and parks.

Finally, we'll delve into the region's love of the supernatural, with ghost stories and legends that will send shivers down your spine. From haunted houses to ghostly apparitions, the Lowcountry is full of eerie tales that have been passed down for generations.

Let's take a journey through the Lowcountry of South Carolina, where you'll discover the stories, trivia, and legends that make this region so unique and beloved.

CHAPTER 1: DISCOVERING THE LOWCOUNTRY

How Did the Lowcountry Get Its Name?

The Lowcountry of South Carolina gets its name from its geography. The region is located in the southern coastal plain of the state, which is characterized by low-lying marshes, estuaries, and barrier islands. The term "Lowcountry" is believed to have originated from the coastal Carolinas and Georgia, where it was used to describe the low-lying areas near the coast.

In addition to the region's physical characteristics, the term "Lowcountry" is also associated with the cultural and historical aspects of the area. The Lowcountry is known for its unique blend of African American heritage, Gullah Geechee culture, and Southern charm, which has shaped the region's traditions, architecture, and cuisine.

Today, the Lowcountry of South Carolina is a popular tourist destination, known for its scenic beauty, rich history, and vibrant culture. Whether you're exploring the region's famous landmarks, savoring its delicious cuisine, or listening to its captivating stories and legends, the Lowcountry is a place that leaves a lasting impression on all who visit.

When Was the Lowcountry Settled?

The Lowcountry of South Carolina was first settled by

Europeans in the late 1600s, with the arrival of English colonists to the region. The first successful English settlement in the area was established in 1670 by a group of settlers led by Sir John Yeamans. The settlement, which was located on the west bank of the Ashley River, was named Charles Town in honor of King Charles II of England.

In the early years of the settlement, the colonists faced a number of challenges, including conflicts with Native American tribes, disease, and food shortages. However, with the labor of enslaved Africans who were brought to the area to work the rice and indigo fields, the colony was able to establish a thriving economy based on agriculture.

Over the next few centuries, the Lowcountry continued to grow and prosper. It became one of the wealthiest regions in the American colonies. The region played a significant role in the American Revolution and the Civil War, with Charleston serving as a major port and strategic location for both conflicts.

Today, the Lowcountry remains a vibrant and culturally rich region, with a rich history that is reflected in its architecture, cuisine, and traditions. Visitors to the area can explore historic landmarks, museums, and other attractions that showcase the region's past, as well as enjoy its natural beauty, outdoor recreation opportunities, and famous southern hospitality.

Geography

The Lowcountry of South Carolina is a region located along the coast of the state, encompassing a wide variety of ecosystems and terrain. The region is characterized by its low-lying geography, with much of the land situated only a few feet above sea level. Here are some of the key features of the Lowcountry's geography:

Coastal Plain - The Lowcountry is located in the southern coastal plain of South Carolina, which extends from the Atlantic Ocean to the Piedmont region of the state.

Barrier Islands - The Lowcountry is home to a series of barrier islands, including Hilton Head Island, Kiawah Island, and Edisto Island. These islands protect the mainland from ocean storms and provide important habitats for wildlife.

Estuaries - The Lowcountry is intersected by numerous rivers and creeks, which flow into the estuaries that are critical to the region's ecology. These estuaries are home to a wide variety of plants and animals, including oysters, crabs, and shrimp.

Marshes - The Lowcountry is also known for its vast marshes, which are characterized by their grassy wetlands and tidal creeks. The marshes provide important habitats for birds, fish, and other wildlife, as well as helping to protect the mainland from coastal erosion and flooding.

Beaches - The Lowcountry is home to a number of beautiful beaches, including Folly Beach, Isle of Palms, and Hunting Island State Park. These beaches are popular destinations for swimming, sunbathing, and outdoor recreation.

Upland Areas - While much of the Lowcountry is low-lying and marshy, there are also some upland areas with rolling hills and forests. These areas provide important habitats for wildlife, as well as opportunities for hiking, camping, and other outdoor activities.

Overall, the geography of the Lowcountry is a unique and diverse landscape that provides a wide variety of habitats for plants and animals, as well as opportunities for outdoor recreation and adventure.

Lowcountry Counties

The Lowcountry of South Carolina is generally considered to encompass a large region of the state, which includes several counties. A county is a geographic and political subdivision of a state. Counties are typically created by state governments to provide local governance and services to residents within a defined geographic area. The exact boundaries of the Lowcountry are somewhat fluid and may vary depending on the context, but here are some of the counties that are typically considered to be part of the Lowcountry:

Beaufort County - Located on the coast between Charleston and Savannah, Beaufort County is known for its historic towns, beautiful beaches, and thriving tourism industry.

Berkeley County - Located north of Charleston, Berkeley County is home to several major military installations and industrial parks, as well as numerous historic sites and parks.

Charleston County - The largest county in the Lowcountry, Charleston County is known for its historic architecture, world-class restaurants, and vibrant arts scene.

Colleton County - Located west of Beaufort County, Colleton County is a largely rural area that is known for its natural beauty and historic landmarks.

Dorchester County - Located northwest of Charleston, Dorchester County is home to several fast-growing communities, as well as numerous historic sites and parks.

Jasper County - Located in the southern Lowcountry between Beaufort County and Savannah, Georgia, Jasper County is known for its natural beauty, historic sites, and unique Gullah Geechee culture.

These counties, along with several others in the region, make up the diverse and fascinating Lowcountry of South Carolina. Each county has its own unique history, culture, and attractions, and together they create a rich tapestry of experiences that make the Lowcountry one of the most captivating and enchanting regions of the United States.

Lowcountry Cities & Towns

The Lowcountry of South Carolina encompasses a large and diverse region that includes several cities and towns. Here are some of the major cities and towns that are typically considered to be part of the Lowcountry:

Charleston - The largest city in the Lowcountry, Charleston is known for its historic architecture, vibrant arts scene, and world-class dining and shopping. The city is also home to several major universities and hospitals, as well as a thriving tourism industry.

Beaufort - Located on the coast between Charleston and Savannah, Beaufort is a charming historic town that features numerous antebellum homes, art galleries, and restaurants.

The town is also home to the Marine Corps Recruit Depot Parris Island, one of the region's major military installations.

Hilton Head Island - A popular resort town located on a barrier island in the southern Lowcountry, Hilton Head Island is known for its beautiful beaches, world-class golf courses, and luxury accommodations.

Mount Pleasant - Located across the Cooper River from Charleston, Mount Pleasant is a fast-growing suburban community that offers easy access to downtown Charleston, as well as numerous parks, restaurants, and shopping centers.

Bluffton - A small town located between Hilton Head Island and Beaufort, Bluffton is known for its charming historic district, riverfront parks, and thriving arts community.

Summerville - Located inland from Charleston, Summerville is a historic town that is known for its beautiful parks, gardens, and historic homes.

These cities and towns, along with many others in the Lowcountry, offer a unique blend of history, culture, and natural beauty that make the region one of the most enchanting and attractive places to live, work, and visit in the United States.

Major Roads and Highways

The Lowcountry of South Carolina is served by several major roads and highways, which connect the region to other parts of the state and beyond. Here are some of the most important roads and highways in the Lowcountry:

I-26 - Interstate 26 is a major east-west highway that runs through the heart of the Lowcountry, connecting Charleston with Columbia and other parts of the state.

I-95 - Interstate 95 runs north-south through the eastern part of the Lowcountry, connecting the region with major cities such as Savannah, Jacksonville, and Miami.

US-17 - US-17 is a major north-south highway that runs along the coast of the Lowcountry, connecting Charleston with other coastal cities and towns such as Beaufort, Hilton Head Island, and Savannah.

US-52 - US-52 is a north-south highway that runs through the center of the Lowcountry, connecting Charleston with other cities and towns such as Moncks Corner, Kingstree, and Florence.

SC-61 - SC-61 is a scenic highway that runs north-south through the Lowcountry, following the Ashley River and connecting Charleston with Summerville, Moncks Corner, and other communities.

SC-170 - SC-170 is an important east-west highway that connects Beaufort with Bluffton and other communities in the southern Lowcountry.

These major roads and highways provide essential transportation links for residents and visitors in the Lowcountry and are an important part of the region's economic and social infrastructure.

Rivers and Waterways

The Lowcountry of South Carolina is home to several major rivers and waterways, which play an important role in the region's ecology, history, and culture. Here are some of the key rivers in the Lowcountry:

Ashley River - a tidal river that flows through Charleston and the surrounding area; known for its scenic beauty and historic landmarks, including Magnolia Plantation and Middleton Place. As the name suggests, the flow and water levels of tidal rivers are controlled by the tide.

Cooper River - a tidal river that flows into Charleston Harbor and is one of the busiest shipping channels on the East Coast; home to the famous Charleston Battery and numerous historic sites.

Edisto River - a blackwater river that flows through the Lowcountry and provides important habitats for fish, wildlife, and plant species; popular for kayaking, fishing, and other outdoor activities. Blackwater rivers flow slowly through swamps and forested wetlands.

Combahee River - a free-flowing blackwater river that originates in the Lowcountry and flows into the St. Helena Sound; known for its diverse range of wildlife and natural beauty.

Waccamaw River - a scenic blackwater river that flows through the Lowcountry and into the Atlantic Ocean. It is known for its lush wetlands and wildlife habitats. Scenic rivers have no dams or man-made obstructions. They have mostly untouched shores and surrounding areas that maintain their natural beauty and wilderness.

Santee River - a major river that flows through the Lowcountry and into the Atlantic Ocean, known for its fishing and boating opportunities; home to the Santee Cooper lakes and numerous state parks.

Intracoastal Waterway - a network of canals and bays that runs along the Atlantic coast, providing a popular route for boaters and commercial vessels. It stretches from Boston, Massachusetts, to Brownsville, Texas.

Kiawah River - a tidal river that flows through Kiawah Island and provides important habitats for wildlife and outdoor recreation opportunities; home to numerous bird species and scenic marshes.

May River - a scenic river that flows through Bluffton and provides popular kayaking and fishing opportunities; known for its beautiful sunset views and historic oyster industry.

St. Helena Sound - an estuary located off the coast of the Lowcountry that provides important habitats for marine life and recreational opportunities for boaters and fishermen; home to numerous barrier islands and beaches.

Overall, the rivers of the Lowcountry are an important part of the region's natural and cultural heritage, providing habitats for wildlife, opportunities for recreation, and a vital link to the region's history and traditions.

Charleston Harbor

Charleston Harbor is a very large and important harbor.

Charleston Harbor is formed by the confluence of the Ashley

and Cooper Rivers, which merge together near the city's downtown area.

The harbor is one of the busiest ports on the East Coast of the United States. It handles a wide range of cargo including automobiles, steel, and chemicals.

Charleston Harbor is home to several major military installations, including the Joint Base Charleston and the Naval Weapons Station.

The harbor played a significant role in the history of the United States. It was a port for the slave trade and the site of the first shots of the Civil War in 1861.

Fort Sumter National Monument, located in Charleston Harbor, is a major tourist attraction and historical site that attracts thousands of visitors each year.

The harbor is also home to several important wildlife habitats, including the Crab Bank Seabird Sanctuary, which is a critical nesting site for several species of seabirds.

The harbor is maintained and managed by the South Carolina Ports Authority, which oversees the operation of several terminals and facilities throughout the region.

Charleston Harbor is one of the deepest natural harbors on the East Coast, with a depth of up to 45 feet in some areas.

The harbor is home to several iconic landmarks, including the Arthur Ravenel Jr. Bridge, which is one of the longest cable-stayed bridges in the world.

The harbor is a popular destination for water sports and recreational activities, including sailing, fishing, kayaking, and paddleboarding.

In addition to its military and commercial uses, Charleston Harbor is also an important site for scientific research, particularly in the areas of marine biology and oceanography.

The harbor is a key location for the transportation of goods and supplies to and from the eastern United States, serving as a major gateway for imports and exports to and from the rest of the world.

Overall, Charleston Harbor is a vital and dynamic hub of activity, serving as an important economic, military, and cultural center for the region and the country as a whole.

Why do People Visit?

The Lowcountry of South Carolina is a popular destination for visitors from around the world, attracting millions of tourists each year. Here are some of the reasons why people visit the Lowcountry:

History and Culture - The Lowcountry has a rich history and unique cultural traditions, including the Gullah Geechee culture, which draws visitors interested in learning more about the region's past and present.

Outdoor Activities - The Lowcountry offers a wide range of outdoor activities, including fishing, boating, kayaking, hiking, and golfing. The region is home to numerous state and national parks, as well as scenic beaches, rivers, and marshes.

Cuisine - The Lowcountry is known for its distinctive cuisine, which blends traditional Southern flavors with seafood and other local ingredients. Visitors come to sample the region's famous dishes, such as shrimp and grits, she-crab soup, and boiled peanuts.

Scenic Beauty - The Lowcountry is home to some of the most beautiful natural scenery in the United States, including pristine beaches, scenic rivers, and lush marshes. Visitors come to enjoy the stunning views and tranquil atmosphere.

Architecture and Landmarks - The Lowcountry is home to numerous historic sites and landmarks, including plantations, forts, and historic homes. Visitors come to explore these sites and learn about the region's rich cultural heritage.

Overall, the Lowcountry offers a unique blend of history, culture, natural beauty, and outdoor adventure that draws visitors from around the world. Whether you're interested in exploring historic landmarks, sampling local cuisine, or simply relaxing on the beach, the Lowcountry has something for everyone.

Famous Landmarks of the Lowcountry

Here are some of the most famous landmarks in the Lowcountry of South Carolina:

Magnolia Plantation and Gardens - One of the oldest and most famous plantations in the South, Magnolia Plantation features beautiful gardens, a plantation house, and a historic slave cabin.

Fort Sumter National Monument - Site of the first shots of the Civil War, Fort Sumter is a must-see destination for history buffs and those interested in the region's rich military history.

Rainbow Row - A series of 13 brightly-colored historic homes in Charleston's historic district, Rainbow Row is one of the most iconic and photographed sites in the city.

The Battery - A historic defensive seawall in Charleston Harbor, the Battery is a popular spot for strolling and sightseeing, offering stunning views of the harbor and the city skyline.

Boone Hall Plantation - A former cotton plantation, Boone Hall features a stunning Avenue of Oaks, historic homes, and scenic gardens.

Charleston City Market - A historic open-air market in downtown Charleston, the Charleston City Market features a wide variety of vendors selling crafts, souvenirs, and local foods.

USS Yorktown - A World War II aircraft carrier that now serves as a museum ship, the USS Yorktown is a popular attraction for visitors interested in military history and naval technology.

Angel Oak - A centuries-old live oak tree on Johns Island, the Angel Oak is a natural wonder and one of the largest and oldest live oak trees in the world.

Harbour Town Lighthouse - Located in the iconic Harbour Town area of Hilton Head Island, the Harbour Town Lighthouse offers stunning views of the island and the surrounding waterways.

Beaufort Historic District - A charming and picturesque district in the town of Beaufort, the Beaufort Historic District features beautifully-preserved antebellum homes, historic churches, and scenic waterfront parks.

Kiawah Island - A beautiful barrier island located south of Charleston, Kiawah Island is known for its luxurious resorts, stunning beaches, and world-class golf courses.

Hunting Island State Park - Located near Beaufort, Hunting Island State Park is a popular destination for hiking, fishing, and beachcombing. The park is also home to a historic lighthouse that offers beautiful views of the surrounding coastline.

Morris Island Lighthouse - Built in 1876, the Morris Island Lighthouse is an iconic landmark located on a small island off the coast of Charleston. The lighthouse is not open to the public but can be seen from nearby beaches and waterways.

Nathaniel Russell House - A beautifully restored historic home in Charleston's historic district, the Nathaniel Russell House offers visitors a glimpse into the lives of Charleston's wealthiest residents during the early 19th century.

Gullah Geechee Cultural Heritage Corridor - A national heritage area that stretches from North Carolina to Florida, the Gullah Geechee Cultural Heritage Corridor is a unique cultural landscape that celebrates the African American culture and traditions of the Lowcountry's Sea Islands. The corridor includes numerous historic sites, museums, and cultural events.

Why Is the Lowcountry Important?

The Lowcountry of South Carolina is an important and

influential region of the state, with a rich history, unique culture, and diverse economy. Here are some of the reasons why the Lowcountry is important to South Carolina:

Economic Impact - The Lowcountry is home to numerous industries and businesses, including tourism, healthcare, education, manufacturing, and shipping. These industries generate billions of dollars in economic activity each year and provide jobs for thousands of South Carolinians.

Cultural Significance - The Lowcountry is a center of African American culture and traditions, with the Gullah Geechee culture being a significant part of the region's heritage. The Lowcountry is also known for its rich culinary traditions, arts and crafts, and historic landmarks, which attract millions of visitors each year.

Political Influence - The Lowcountry is home to several important political leaders and institutions, including the City of Charleston, which is the state's largest and most influential city. The Lowcountry also has a significant military presence, with several major military installations located throughout the region.

Environmental Importance - The Lowcountry is home to some of the most important and fragile ecosystems in the United States, including tidal creeks, salt marshes, and barrier islands. These ecosystems provide important habitats for a diverse range of wildlife and plant species, as well as essential ecological services, such as storm protection and water filtration.

Overall, the Lowcountry is a vital and influential region of South Carolina and the rest of the United States of America, with a unique identity and important contributions to the state's economy, culture, politics, and environment.

CHAPTER 2: ROOTS AND RESILIENCE: THE RICH HISTORY AND VIBRANT CULTURE OF THE LOWCOUNTRY

A Short History

The Lowcountry of South Carolina has a rich and complex history that stretches back thousands of years. The region's earliest inhabitants were indigenous peoples, including the Edisto, Waccamaw, and Catawba tribes, who lived off the land and waterways of the region. These Native American cultures left behind a rich legacy of art, language, and traditions that continue to be celebrated today.

In the early 16th century, Spanish explorers arrived in the Lowcountry and claimed the region for Spain. However, it was not until the 1670s that European settlers established a permanent presence in the region, with the founding of the city of Charleston in 1670.

Throughout the colonial era and into the 19th century, the Lowcountry was dominated by large plantations that relied on enslaved labor to produce rice, indigo, and other cash crops. The wealth generated by these plantations allowed Charleston to become one of the wealthiest cities in the United States, and the Lowcountry to become a cultural and economic center of the South.

The Civil War had a profound impact on the Lowcountry, as the region was the site of many important battles and experienced significant damage and destruction. Following the war, the region struggled to rebuild, and the plantation economy collapsed. However, the Lowcountry remained an important center of African American culture and traditions, with the Gullah Geechee people preserving many of their unique cultural practices and language.

In the 20th century, the Lowcountry began to experience significant growth and development, with Charleston and other cities becoming popular tourist destinations and centers of industry and commerce. Today, the Lowcountry is a thriving and vibrant region that continues to celebrate its rich history and unique culture, while embracing new opportunities and challenges for the future.

Lowcountry Culture

The culture of the Lowcountry of South Carolina is a rich and complex blend of traditions that reflect the region's diverse history and unique geography. The Lowcountry is known for its distinctive Gullah Geechee culture, which has its roots in the enslaved Africans who were brought to the region to work on the rice plantations.

The Gullah Geechee people have a distinct language, foodways, music, and art that reflect their African heritage and the unique circumstances of their enslavement and subsequent isolation on the Sea Islands of the Lowcountry. Today, the Gullah Geechee culture is celebrated and preserved through cultural events, museums, and community organizations.

In addition to the Gullah Geechee culture, the Lowcountry is known for its rich culinary traditions, which blend traditional Southern flavors with seafood and other local ingredients. Dishes such as shrimp and grits, she-crab soup, and Lowcountry boil are staples of the region's cuisine, and are popular with locals and visitors alike.

The Lowcountry is also known for its vibrant arts scene, with numerous galleries, theaters, and performance spaces showcasing the work of local artists and performers. The region has a long tradition of arts and crafts, including sweetgrass basket weaving, which is practiced by many Gullah Geechee artisans.

Religion also plays an important role in the culture of the Lowcountry, with numerous historic churches and religious landmarks located throughout the region. Christianity, particularly the Episcopal and Baptist faiths, has a strong presence in the region, but there are also numerous other religious traditions represented.

The Lowcountry is also home to a large military presence, with several major military installations located throughout the region. The military culture has had a significant impact on the Lowcountry's history and identity, with numerous landmarks and memorials dedicated to the region's military heritage.

The Lowcountry also has a significant Jewish population, with numerous synagogues and Jewish cultural organizations located throughout the region. Jewish culture and traditions have played an important role in the Lowcountry's history and identity and have contributed to the region's diversity and vibrancy.

Overall, the culture of the Lowcountry is a rich and diverse tapestry of traditions and practices that reflect the region's complex history and unique identity. From its vibrant arts scene to its delicious cuisine and rich cultural heritage, the Lowcountry has something to offer everyone who visits or calls this enchanting region home.

The People

The Lowcountry of South Carolina is a region that has been shaped by a wide variety of cultural and ethnic influences over the years. Some of the major groups that have settled the Lowcountry include:

English - English settlers were some of the earliest Europeans to establish a presence in the Lowcountry, with the founding of the Carolina colony in 1670.

French Huguenots - French Huguenots, who were Protestant refugees from France, established settlements in the Lowcountry in the late 1600s and early 1700s.

Spanish - Spanish explorers and settlers also made their mark on the Lowcountry, with the establishment of missions and settlements in the 16th and 17th centuries.

Gullah Geechee - The Gullah Geechee are a unique cultural group that is descended from enslaved Africans who were brought to the Lowcountry in the 18th and 19th centuries. They have their own distinct language, cuisine, and cultural practices.

African Americans - African Americans have played a vital role in the history and culture of the Lowcountry, both as enslaved persons and as free citizens.

Native Americans - Several Native American tribes have

inhabited the Lowcountry for thousands of years, including the Cherokee, Catawba, and Yemassee peoples.

Irish - Irish immigrants began arriving in the Lowcountry in the early 19th century and have contributed to the region's cultural and economic development.

German - German immigrants also settled in the Lowcountry in the 18th and 19th centuries, bringing with them their own cultural traditions and contributions.

Scottish - Scottish immigrants arrived in the Lowcountry in the 18th century, and their influence can be seen in the region's architecture, music, and cultural traditions.

Jewish - Jewish immigrants have been a part of the Lowcountry's cultural fabric since the colonial period, and have contributed to the region's religious, economic, and social life.

Italian - Italian immigrants arrived in the Lowcountry in the late 19th and early 20th centuries and have made significant contributions to the region's cuisine and cultural life.

Lebanese - Lebanese immigrants began arriving in the Lowcountry in the late 19th century and have made important contributions to the region's economic and cultural development.

Overall, the Lowcountry is a diverse and multicultural region that has been shaped by a wide variety of cultural and ethnic influences over the years. This rich cultural heritage is an important part of the region's identity and character.

Historic Moments

Founding of Charles Town - 1670: English colonists led by Sir John Yeamans established the first successful English settlement in the Lowcountry, which was later named Charles Town.

Stono Rebellion - 1739: Enslaved Africans led a revolt against their masters near the Stono River, resulting in the deaths of dozens of people and even harsher slave laws.

Siege of Charleston - 1780: British forces, led by General Sir Henry Clinton, attacked, and then captured the city of Charleston during the American Revolution, resulting in the city being occupied for several years.

South Carolina's ratification of the US Constitution - 1788: South Carolina became the eighth state to ratify the US Constitution, which established the framework for the new federal government.

Nullification Crisis - 1832: South Carolina declared federal tariffs unconstitutional and threatened to secede from the Union, leading to a standoff with the federal government.

Secession Convention - 1860: South Carolina held a convention that voted to secede from the Union, becoming the first state to do so.

Civil War Battle of Fort Sumter - 1861: Confederate forces attacked and captured Fort Sumter, marking the beginning of the Civil War.

Reconstruction Era - 1865-1877: Following the end of the Civil War, the federal government oversaw a period of Reconstruction in which former slaves were granted citizenship and other rights.

Hurricane of 1893 - 1893: A massive hurricane struck the Lowcountry, causing widespread devastation and claiming over 2,000 lives.

Charleston Earthquake - 1886: An earthquake struck Charleston, causing significant damage to buildings and infrastructure, and resulting in over 100 deaths.

Charleston Hospital Strike - 1969: African American hospital workers in Charleston went on strike to demand better pay and working conditions, marking a significant moment in the civil rights movement.

Hurricane Hugo - 1989: A powerful hurricane struck the Lowcountry, causing widespread damage and claiming over 30 lives.

The Lowcountry and the US Military

The Lowcountry of South Carolina is home to several important military establishments, including:

Joint Base Charleston - Located near North Charleston, Joint Base Charleston is a major military installation that serves as the home of the 628th Air Base Wing, the 437th Airlift Wing, and the 315th Airlift Wing. The base is an important hub for military transportation and logistics, with numerous aircraft and personnel stationed there.

Marine Corps Recruit Depot Parris Island - Located near Beaufort, Parris Island is the home of the Marine Corps Recruit Training Center, where all female enlisted Marines and all male recruits from east of the Mississippi River undergo basic training.

Naval Weapons Station Charleston- Located on the west bank of the Cooper River, Naval Weapons Station Charleston is a major military installation that provides support for the U.S. Navy's Atlantic Fleet. The base is home to numerous military units and facilities, including a naval hospital and a naval brig.

Coast Guard Sector Charleston - Located in downtown Charleston, Coast Guard Sector Charleston is responsible for maritime safety and security in the Lowcountry region. The sector provides search and rescue services, enforces maritime laws and regulations, and supports other Coast Guard missions.

These military establishments have a significant impact on the Lowcountry's economy and culture and are an important part of the region's history and identity.

Military Monuments

The Lowcountry of South Carolina is home to several important military monuments and memorials, including:

Fort Sumter National Monument - Site of the first shots of the Civil War, Fort Sumter is a major military monument that attracts thousands of visitors each year. The fort is located on an island in Charleston Harbor and can be reached by boat.

Patriots Point Naval & Maritime Museum - Located in Mount Pleasant, Patriots Point is a major military museum and monument that showcases the history of the U.S. Navy and the role of South Carolina in the nation's military history. The museum is home to several historic naval vessels, including the aircraft carrier USS Yorktown, and features numerous exhibits and displays.

The Citadel War Memorial - Located on the campus of The Citadel military college in Charleston, the Citadel War Memorial is a monument to the school's alumni who have lost their lives in military service. The monument includes the names of more than 600 Citadel graduates who have died in wars and military conflicts throughout history.

Battery Park - Located on the tip of the Charleston peninsula, Battery Park is a historic military monument that features a seawall and several artillery batteries that were used to defend the city during times of war. The park offers stunning views of the harbor and the city skyline and is a popular spot for strolling and sightseeing.

Beaufort National Cemetery - Located in Beaufort, the Beaufort National Cemetery is a military cemetery that honors the sacrifices of U.S. service members who have died in the line of duty. The cemetery features rows of white headstones, a chapel, and several monuments and memorials.

These military monuments and memorials are important reminders of the sacrifices made by U.S. service members throughout history and serve as a testament to the region's rich military heritage.

More Lowcountry History

The first golf course in America was established in the Lowcountry in 1786 on Harleston Green in Charleston.

In the 1920s, the Lowcountry was a hub for moonshining and bootlegging during Prohibition, with illegal liquor stills hidden in remote areas of the region.

The Charleston Battery, a historic defensive seawall in Charleston Harbor, was built in 1818 and is now a popular spot for sunset strolls and picnics.

The Lowcountry was a popular location for pirate hideouts and battles during the Golden Age of Piracy in the early 18th century.

The sweetgrass basket weaving tradition, which is still practiced today, originated in West Africa and was brought to the Lowcountry by enslaved Africans in the 17th century.

The Charleston Renaissance, a cultural and artistic movement that took place in the 1920s and 1930s, produced renowned writers like DuBose Heyward and artists like Alice Ravenel Huger Smith.

The Lowcountry is home to a number of historic plantations, including Magnolia Plantation and Gardens, which was founded in 1676 and is one of the oldest public gardens in America.

The Lowcountry is also known for its unique Gullah Geechee culture, which originated with enslaved Africans in the region and is characterized by its own dialect, cuisine, music, and traditions.

The Lowcountry was a key location in the Civil Rights Movement, with notable figures like Septima Clark and Esau Jenkins working to secure voting rights and desegregation in the region.

The Lowcountry has a long history of religious diversity, with significant Jewish, Catholic, and Protestant communities coexisting in the region for centuries.

Lowcountry Inventions

The Lowcountry of South Carolina has a rich history of innovation and invention. Here are some examples of notable inventions that were developed in the Lowcountry:

The Rice Cultivation System - In the 18th and 19th centuries, enslaved Africans in the Lowcountry developed a sophisticated system of cultivating rice, which became one of the region's most profitable and important crops.

The Charleston Battery - The Charleston Battery, a historic defensive seawall in Charleston Harbor, was constructed in 1818 to protect the city from naval attacks.

The Submarine - The H.L. Hunley, a submarine built in the Lowcountry during the Civil War, was the first submarine to successfully sink an enemy ship.

The Pinckney Drafting Table - The Pinckney Drafting Table, invented by South Carolina native Charles Pinckney in the 1820s, was a portable table used for drafting maps and architectural drawings.

The Sweetgrass Basket - The sweetgrass basket weaving

tradition, which is still practiced in the Lowcountry today, originated with enslaved Africans in the 17th century and is now considered a distinct art form.

The Charleston Receipts Cookbook - The Charleston Receipts cookbook, first published in 1950 by the Junior League of Charleston, popularized Lowcountry cuisine and helped to establish Charleston as a culinary destination.

The Charleston Earthquake Detector - The Charleston Earthquake Detector, invented by South Carolina native John Wesley Hyatt in the late 19th century, was an early seismometer that could detect earthquakes and other seismic activity.

The Marsh Tacky Horse - The Marsh Tacky horse, a breed of horse that is native to the Lowcountry and was once used for work on rice plantations, is now being bred and preserved as part of the region's cultural heritage.

The Automatic Gate - The first automatic gate was invented by Joseph Bramah, a British engineer who owned a plantation in South Carolina. The gate used water pressure to automatically open and close. It was patented in 1798.

The Printing Press - The first printing press in South Carolina was brought to Charleston in 1730 by a printer named Lewis Timothy. The press was used to print newspapers, books, and other materials that helped to disseminate knowledge and ideas throughout the region.

The Firefly Lighter - The Firefly lighter, which uses a battery-powered heating element to ignite a flame, was invented by a South Carolina entrepreneur named Phil Davison in the early 2000s. The lighter quickly became popular for its convenience and reliability.

The Vertical-Lift Bridge - The Arthur Ravenel Jr. Bridge, which spans the Cooper River in Charleston, is a modern engineering marvel that features a unique vertical-lift design. The bridge, which was completed in 2005, has become an iconic symbol of the Lowcountry.

The Stingray Shuffle - The Stingray Shuffle is a technique for wading safely in the shallow waters of the Lowcountry, where stingrays are common. The technique involves shuffling your feet along the bottom of the water to avoid stepping on a hidden stingray, which can cause a painful and potentially dangerous sting. The Stingray Shuffle is now widely recognized as an important safety tip for anyone swimming or wading in the Lowcountry's waters.

These are just a few examples of the many important inventions and innovations that have emerged from the Lowcountry of South Carolina over the years.

CHAPTER 3 PRESERVING THE PAST: MUSEUMS OF THE LOWCOUNTRY

The Lowcountry is home to a remarkable collection of museums that offer windows into the past, present, and future of this unique corner of the world.

The Charleston Museum

The Charleston Museum, located in the heart of Charleston, holds a special place in the region's history and culture. It is believed to be America's first museum. It stands as a testament to the enduring significance of preserving and sharing the stories of the past.

The museum's extensive collections cover a wide range of subjects, including Charleston's history, natural history, decorative arts, and more. Its exhibits offer a deep dive into the city's past, showcasing artifacts that illuminate the diverse aspects of Charleston's cultural and historical identity. From Native American artifacts and colonial-era objects to Civil War memorabilia and Gullah Geechee heritage, the museum presents a comprehensive narrative of the region's past, offering invaluable insights into its development and complexities.

From the impacts of slavery and the plantation economy to the contributions of African Americans and the evolution of Charleston's vibrant arts scene, the museum provides a multifaceted perspective on the city's past and present.

The Gibbes Museum of Art

The Gibbes Museum is renowned for its focus on American art, with a particular emphasis on Southern art and its profound influence on the region. Its collection spans centuries and encompasses a wide range of mediums, including paintings, sculptures, photographs, and works on paper. Visitors are treated to a vibrant showcase of artistic expressions, from traditional to contemporary, reflecting the diverse stories and perspectives of the Lowcountry and beyond.

One of the key reasons to visit the Gibbes Museum is the opportunity to immerse oneself in the rich artistic traditions of the South. The museum's curated exhibits not only feature works by acclaimed Southern artists but also delve into the cultural and historical contexts that have shaped their creations. From landscapes that capture the ethereal beauty of the Lowcountry to thought-provoking pieces that explore social issues and identity, the museum offers a platform for meaningful conversations and connections with art.

Beyond its remarkable collection, the Gibbes Museum is a hub of cultural engagement and education. The museum hosts a variety of events, including artist talks, workshops, and performances, which offer opportunities for deeper insights and creative exploration. It also provides educational programs for all ages, fostering a love of art and encouraging artistic expression among the community.

Charleston Museum Homes

Charleston also has a unique collection of museum homes. They stand as living testaments to the past, inviting visitors to step into the elegant world of Charleston's storied residents. These beautifully preserved homes provide a glimpse into the lives of those who shaped the city's history and offer a captivating blend of architectural splendor, period furnishings, and captivating narratives.

Among the notable museum homes in Charleston is the Nathaniel Russell House. This exquisite Federal-style mansion showcases the opulence of the early 19th century. It features a grand double staircase, intricate plasterwork, and stunning collection of decorative arts. As visitors wander through its meticulously restored rooms, they can imagine the bustling social gatherings and the daily lives of the Russell family, gaining insight into Charleston's vibrant past.

Another gem is the Aiken-Rhett House, a carefully preserved antebellum townhouse that offers a rare glimpse into the everyday lives of both the wealthy and the enslaved who lived within its walls. Uniquely presented in an "as-is" state, the house allows visitors to see the layers of history and evolution over time, offering a deeper understanding of the complexities of Southern society.

The Heyward-Washington House, located in the heart of Charleston's historic district, tells the stories of two prominent figures in American history: Thomas Heyward Jr., a signer of the Declaration of Independence, and George Washington, who stayed at the house during his presidential visit to the city. This Georgian-style home features period furniture, beautiful gardens, and a captivating blend of

American and British decorative arts.

Each museum home in Charleston showcases a distinct architectural style and reflects a different era in the city's history. They collectively provide an intimate and tangible connection to the past, allowing visitors to immerse themselves in the charm, sophistication, and sometimes complex narratives of Charleston's storied past. With their carefully preserved interiors, period furnishings, and knowledgeable guides, these museum homes offer a fascinating journey through time, capturing the spirit of a bygone era and illuminating the multi-faceted history of Charleston.

The International African American Museum

One of the newest museums in the area is the International African American Museum (IAAM). It is cultural institution that honors the history, contributions, and experiences of African Americans. The museum engages visitors in a comprehensive exploration of African American history, from the transatlantic slave trade to the present day.

The IAAM is situated on the site known as Gadsden's Wharf, where an estimated 40% of enslaved Africans arrived in America.

The museum's exhibits offer a multi-dimensional journey through time, weaving together personal narratives, archival materials, interactive displays, and cutting-edge technology. Visitors are invited to explore the untold stories of resilience, resistance, and triumph, showcasing the contributions of

African Americans in various fields, including art, music, literature, science, politics, and civil rights activism.

The IAAM also delves into the complex and nuanced history of the Gullah Geechee culture, which originated from the West African roots of enslaved Africans in the Lowcountry region. Through immersive exhibits and interpretive programs, visitors can gain a deeper understanding of the Gullah Geechee heritage, language, traditions, and enduring cultural influence.

The museum aims to create a space where visitors of all backgrounds can engage in conversations about race, identity, and equality, promoting a more inclusive and compassionate society.

Maritime and Military Museums

The Lowcountry of South Carolina boasts a rich maritime and military heritage. Its museums provide a window into this storied past. From naval history to pivotal moments of conflict, these institutions offer immersive experiences that honor the region's maritime and military traditions.

The Patriots Point Naval & Maritime Museum, located in Mount Pleasant, is a prominent destination for history enthusiasts and naval enthusiasts alike. The museum is anchored by the majestic USS Yorktown, an aircraft carrier that played a significant role in World War II. Visitors can explore the ship's expansive deck, venture into its compartments, and discover firsthand the challenges faced by sailors at sea. The museum also includes a destroyer, the USS Laffey, and a submarine, the USS Clamagore, providing a comprehensive exploration of naval history.

Fort Sumter National Monument, located on a small island in Charleston Harbor, is an iconic site associated with the beginning of the American Civil War. The fort witnessed the first shots of the conflict in 1861, and today, visitors can take a boat tour to the fort to experience its historic significance. Through exhibits, guided tours, and interpretive programs, visitors gain insights into the events leading up to the war and the impact it had on the nation.

These maritime and military museums offer immersive experiences that transport visitors to pivotal moments in history. Whether exploring the decks of a historic aircraft carrier, learning about the events that led to the Civil War, or delving into the military heritage of South Carolina, visitors are invited to reflect on the bravery, sacrifice, and resilience of those who served.

Natural History Museums

Natural history museums in the Lowcountry play a vital role in preserving and showcasing the region's unique flora, fauna, geology, and ecosystems. These museums offer visitors a fascinating glimpse into the natural wonders that make the Lowcountry a truly remarkable destination.

One notable natural history museum in the region is the Mace Brown Museum of Natural History, located at the College of Charleston. This museum houses extensive collections of fossils, minerals, plants, and animals, providing a comprehensive exploration of the Lowcountry's natural history. Visitors can marvel at the ancient fossils that reveal the region's prehistoric past, discover the intricate beauty of minerals, and learn about the diverse plant and animal species that call the Lowcountry home.

The Coastal Discovery Museum, located on Hilton Head Island, is another prominent institution that celebrates the natural history of the Lowcountry. This museum offers exhibits, interactive displays, and outdoor programs that allow visitors to explore and learn about the unique coastal ecosystems, marshlands, and wildlife that thrive in the area. From coastal birds and sea turtles to tidal habitats and the intricate web of life in the salt marshes, the Coastal Discovery Museum provides a fascinating experience for nature enthusiasts of all ages.

In addition to these museums, the Lowcountry is home to a network of nature centers, wildlife refuges, and educational organizations that promote environmental conservation and provide opportunities for outdoor exploration. The Center for Birds of Prey, located in Awendaw, focuses on the conservation of birds of prey and offers educational programs and live bird demonstrations. The ACE Basin National Wildlife Refuge, encompassing vast expanses of wetlands and forested areas, provides habitats for numerous species of wildlife and offers opportunities for birdwatching, hiking, and wildlife photography.

These natural history museums and centers not only showcase the beauty and diversity of the Lowcountry's natural environment but also educate visitors about the importance of conservation and sustainability. They serve as hubs for research, environmental advocacy, and educational programs that inspire a deeper appreciation for the region's natural heritage and foster a sense of stewardship for future generations.

CHAPTER 4 FAMOUS PEOPLE OF THE LOWCOUNTY

Historical Figures

The Lowcountry of South Carolina has been home to many notable historical figures over the years. Here are just a few examples:

Robert Smalls - Robert Smalls was an enslaved man who escaped to freedom by commandeering a Confederate ship in Charleston Harbor during the Civil War. He went on to serve as a Union Navy captain and later a U.S. Congressman.

Charles Cotesworth Pinckney - Charles Cotesworth Pinckney was a Founding Father of the United States and a prominent lawyer and politician from South Carolina. He was a delegate to the Constitutional Convention and played a key role in drafting the U.S. Constitution.

Harriet Tubman - Harriet Tubman was an abolitionist and activist who helped free hundreds of enslaved people through the Underground Railroad. She spent time in Beaufort, South Carolina during the Civil War, where she served as a nurse, spy, and scout for the Union Army.

Septima Clark - Septima Clark was an educator and civil rights activist who played a key role in the desegregation of public schools in Charleston. She also helped establish Citizenship Schools, which taught literacy and other skills to Black adults who had been denied an education under segregation.

Pat Conroy - Pat Conroy was a beloved author who wrote several novels set in the Lowcountry, including "The Great Santini," "The Lords of Discipline," and "The Prince of Tides."

John C. Calhoun - John C. Calhoun was a prominent statesman and politician from South Carolina who served as Vice President of the United States under John Quincy Adams and Andrew Jackson. He was a staunch defender of states' rights and slavery, and his views helped fuel tensions leading up to the Civil War.

Mary McLeod Bethune - Mary McLeod Bethune was a prominent educator and civil rights leader who founded the National Council of Negro Women and served as an advisor to President Franklin D. Roosevelt.

DuBose Heyward - DuBose Heyward was a writer who is best known for his novel "Porgy," which was later adapted into the opera "Porgy and Bess" by George Gershwin.

Thomas Heyward Jr. - Thomas Heyward Jr. was a Founding Father of the United States and a signer of the Declaration of Independence. He was born in St. Luke's Parish in the Lowcountry.

Robert Barnwell Rhett - Robert Barnwell Rhett was a politician and newspaper editor who was one of the leading voices of the secession movement in the years leading up to the Civil War.

Angelina and Sarah Grimké - Angelina and Sarah Grimké were sisters who were born in Charleston and became prominent abolitionists and women's rights activists in the 19th century.

Alice Childress - Alice Childress was a playwright and actress who wrote several plays that explored issues of race and gender. She was born in Charleston.

William Gilmore Simms - William Gilmore Simms was a writer and literary figure who lived in Charleston and wrote extensively about the history and culture of the Lowcountry.

John Rutledge - John Rutledge was a Founding Father of the United States and a prominent lawyer and politician from South Carolina. He served as the second Chief Justice of the United States and was a delegate to the Constitutional Convention.

John Laurens - John Laurens was a Revolutionary War soldier from South Carolina who fought to end slavery and promote civil rights for Black Americans. He was killed in action in 1782.

Actors and Actresses

The Lowcountry has been the birthplace or home to many talented actors and actresses over the years. Here are a few:

Bill Murray - Bill Murray is a comedian and actor who was born in Evanston, Illinois, but spent much of his childhood in Charleston, South Carolina. He is known for his roles in films such as "Ghostbusters," "Groundhog Day," and "Lost in Translation."

Darius Rucker - Darius Rucker is a musician and actor who was born and raised in Charleston, South Carolina. He is best known as the lead singer of the band Hootie & the Blowfish and has also had success as a solo artist.

Stephen Colbert - Stephen Colbert is a comedian, writer, and actor who was born in Washington, D.C., but grew up in Charleston, South Carolina. He is best known as the host of "The Colbert Report" and "The Late Show with Stephen Colbert."

Thomas Gibson - Thomas Gibson is an actor who was born in Charleston, South Carolina. He is best known for his roles in television series such as "Dharma & Greg" and "Criminal Minds."

Eliza Limehouse - Eliza Limehouse is a reality TV personality who was born and raised in Charleston, South Carolina. She appeared on the Bravo series "Southern Charm."

Musicians

Darius Rucker isn't the only musician who has called Charleston, South Carolina home. The Lowcountry has been home to many famous musicians over the years. Here are some others:

Bill Withers - Bill Withers was a singer and songwriter who was born in Slab Fork, West Virginia, but later moved to Charleston, South Carolina. He is best known for his hit songs "Ain't No Sunshine," "Lean on Me," and "Lovely Day."

The Charleston Symphony Orchestra - The Charleston Symphony Orchestra is a professional orchestra based in Charleston, South Carolina. Founded in 1936, it has become one of the premier orchestras in the southeastern United States.

Ranky Tanky - Ranky Tanky is a Charleston-based musical

group that performs Gullah music, a style of music that originated in the Lowcountry of South Carolina and Georgia. The group has won critical acclaim for their unique sound and powerful performances.

Mark Bryan - Mark Bryan is a musician and songwriter who is best known as the lead guitarist for Hootie & the Blowfish. He is also a solo artist and has released several albums of his own music.

Charlton Singleton - Charlton Singleton is a jazz trumpeter and composer who was born and raised in Awendaw, South Carolina, just outside of Charleston. He is a member of the Charleston Jazz Orchestra and has performed with a variety of musicians and groups over the years.

Jake Shimabukuro - Jake Shimabukuro is a ukulele virtuoso who was born in Honolulu, Hawaii, but now resides in Charleston, South Carolina. He is known for his incredible skill and versatility on the ukulele and has become one of the instrument's most popular and innovative performers.

These are just a few examples of the many talented musicians who have called Charleston, South Carolina home over the years.

Writers

The Lowcountry has been home to many talented writers over the years. Here are some examples:

Pat Conroy - Pat Conroy was a novelist and memoirist who was born and raised in Beaufort, South Carolina, just outside of Charleston. He is best known for his novels "The Prince of

Tides" and "The Great Santini."

Josephine Humphreys - Josephine Humphreys is a novelist who was born and raised in Charleston, South Carolina. Her best-known works include "Rich in Love" and "Nowhere Else on Earth."

Dubose Heyward - Dubose Heyward was a novelist and playwright who was born and raised in Charleston, South Carolina. He is best known for his novel "Porgy," which was later adapted into the opera "Porgy and Bess" by George Gershwin.

Mary Alice Monroe - Mary Alice Monroe is a novelist who was born and raised in the Lowcountry of South Carolina. Her best-known works include the "Lowcountry Summer" series and "The Beach House."

Sue Monk Kidd - Sue Monk Kidd is a novelist who was born in Sylvester, Georgia, but has lived in Charleston, South Carolina, for many years. Her best-known works include "The Secret Life of Bees" and "The Invention of Wings."

William Gilmore Simms - William Gilmore Simms was a writer and literary figure who lived in Charleston and wrote extensively about the history and culture of the Lowcountry.

Anne Rivers Siddons - Anne Rivers Siddons was a novelist who was born and raised in Atlanta, Georgia, but lived in Charleston, South Carolina, for many years. Her best-known works include "Peachtree Road" and "The House Next Door."

John Bennett - John Bennett is a poet, novelist, and essayist who was born and raised in Charleston, South Carolina. He is known for his powerful and evocative writing about the natural world and the human experience.

E. Lee Spence - E. Lee Spence is a historian and writer who has lived and worked in Charleston, South Carolina, for many years. He is best known for his work on the history and archaeology of shipwrecks off the coast of the Lowcountry.

Frank Gilbreth - Frank Gilbreth was an industrial engineer and writer who was born and raised in Charleston, South Carolina. He is best known for his book "Cheaper by the Dozen," which he co-wrote with his wife, Lillian.

Julia Peterkin - Julia Peterkin was a novelist and short story writer who lived in the Lowcountry of South Carolina for many years. She is best known for her novel "Scarlet Sister Mary," which won the Pulitzer Prize in 1929.

These are just a few examples of the many talented writers who have called Charleston and the surrounding areas home over the years.

Politicians

The Lowcountry has been home to many notable politicians over the years. Here are some examples of famous politicians from the area:

John C. Calhoun - John C. Calhoun was a statesman and political theorist who was born in Abbeville, South Carolina, but lived in Charleston for much of his life. He served as Vice President of the United States under both John Quincy Adams and Andrew Jackson.

Arthur Ravenel Jr. - Arthur Ravenel Jr. was a politician and businessman who was born and raised in Charleston, South Carolina. He served in the South Carolina House of

Representatives and later represented the state's 1st Congressional District in the U.S. House of Representatives.

Strom Thurmond - Strom Thurmond was a politician and attorney who was born in Edgefield, South Carolina, but later lived in Charleston. He served as Governor of South Carolina and later represented the state in the U.S. Senate for over 48 years.

Robert B. Rhett - Robert B. Rhett was a journalist and politician who lived in Charleston, South Carolina, during the mid-19th century. He was a prominent advocate of states' rights and secession leading up to the Civil War.

John Rutledge - John Rutledge was a lawyer and politician who was born in Charleston, South Carolina, in 1739. He served as the state's first Governor and later became Chief Justice of the United States Supreme Court.

Joseph P. Riley Jr. - Joseph P. Riley Jr. was a politician who was born and raised in Charleston, South Carolina. He served as the city's mayor for 40 years, from 1975 to 2016, and is widely credited with revitalizing the city's downtown area.

Lindsey Graham - Lindsey Graham is a politician and attorney who was born in Central, South Carolina, but later moved to the Charleston area. He has served as a U.S. Senator from South Carolina since 2003 and is known for his conservative views.

Tim Scott - Tim Scott is a politician and businessman who was born in North Charleston, South Carolina. He has served as a U.S. Senator from South Carolina since 2013 and is the first African American senator to be elected from the state.

Jenny Sanford - Jenny Sanford is a businesswoman and

former First Lady of South Carolina. She was born in Winnetka, Illinois, but later moved to Charleston, South Carolina, with her family. Her ex-husband, Mark Sanford, served as Governor of South Carolina from 2003 to 2011.

Nancy Mace - Nancy Mace is a politician and businesswoman who was born and raised in Charleston, South Carolina. She was elected to represent the state's 1st Congressional District in the U.S. House of Representatives in 2020.

Joe Cunningham - Joe Cunningham is a politician and attorney who was born and raised in Charleston, South Carolina. He served as the U.S. Representative for the state's 1st Congressional District from 2019 to 2021.

These politicians have made significant contributions to the political landscape of the United States and have helped to put Charleston and the surrounding areas on the map as a hub for political activity and influence.

Athletes

The Lowcountry has also been home to a few famous athletes.

Stephen Davis - Stephen Davis is a former NFL running back who was born in Spartanburg, SC, but grew up in Summerville, SC, just outside of Charleston. He played for the Carolina Panthers, the St. Louis Rams, and the Washington Redskins during his career.

Alshon Jeffery - Alshon Jeffery is a wide receiver in the NFL who was born in St. Matthews, SC, but attended high school in Calhoun County, SC, which is just outside of Charleston. He has played for the Chicago Bears, the Philadelphia Eagles, and the Cleveland Browns.

Robert Porcher - Robert Porcher is a former NFL defensive end who was born in Cheraw, SC, but grew up in Wando, SC, which is just outside of Charleston. He played for the Detroit Lions for his entire career and was named to three Pro Bowls.

Troy Brown - Troy Brown is a former NFL wide receiver who was born in Barnwell, SC, but attended high school in Ridgeville, SC, which is just outside of Charleston. He played for the New England Patriots for his entire career and was named to one Pro Bowl.

Bill Sharpe - Bill Sharpe is a former professional golfer who was born and raised in Greenville, SC, but currently lives in Charleston. He played on the PGA Tour in the 1980s and 1990s and is now a golf instructor and commentator.

Matthew Roberts - Matthew Roberts is a former professional soccer player who was born and raised in Charleston, SC. He played for the Charleston Battery and several other professional teams during his career.

CHAPTER 5 HAUNTED HISTORY: SUPERNATURAL TALES FROM THE LOWCOUNTRY

The Lowcountry is steeped in history and has been the site of numerous supernatural events over the years. From haunted buildings to ghostly apparitions, the area's haunted history is rich and fascinating.

Haunted Places

Whether you're a believer in the supernatural or not, these stories and legends about haunted places are a fascinating aspect of the area's rich history and culture.

Old City Jail (Charleston) - As mentioned before, the Old City Jail is known for its harsh conditions and the many prisoners who died there. Visitors have reported seeing ghostly apparitions and hearing strange noises within its walls.

Magnolia Plantation and Gardens (Charleston) - Magnolia Plantation is said to be haunted by the ghosts of former slaves and soldiers who died on the property during the Civil War. Visitors have reported seeing ghostly figures and experiencing strange occurrences in the gardens and on the grounds.

Poogan's Porch Restaurant (Charleston) - Poogan's Porch is housed in a historic building that is said to be haunted by the ghost of a former resident named Zoe St. Amand. Visitors have reported seeing her ghostly figure in the restaurant and feeling her presence.

The Battery Carriage House Inn (Charleston) - As mentioned before, the Battery Carriage House Inn is said to be haunted by the ghost of a former resident. Visitors have reported seeing ghostly apparitions and hearing strange noises in the building.

Circular Congregational Church (Charleston) - The Circular Congregational Church is said to be haunted by the ghosts of former congregants and slaves who were buried in the church's cemetery. Visitors have reported seeing ghostly apparitions and hearing strange noises in the church.

The Heyward-Washington House (Charleston) - This historic house is said to be haunted by the ghost of a former owner named Thomas Heyward Jr. Visitors have reported seeing his ghostly figure in the house.

The Old Exchange and Provost Dungeon (Charleston) - The Old Exchange and Provost Dungeon served as a prison during the Revolutionary War and is said to be haunted by the ghosts of former prisoners. Visitors have reported hearing strange noises and feeling an eerie presence in the dungeon.

The Mills House Hotel (Charleston) - The Mills House Hotel is said to be haunted by the ghost of a former maid who died in a fire in the hotel in the 1800s. Visitors have reported seeing her ghostly figure and feeling her presence.

The Ghost Bridge (Beaufort) - The Ghost Bridge is said to be haunted by the ghosts of former slaves who were hung from the bridge during the Civil War. Visitors have reported seeing ghostly figures and experiencing strange occurrences near the bridge.

The Battery (Charleston) - The Battery is a historic landmark in Charleston and is said to be haunted by the ghosts of former soldiers and sailors. Visitors have reported seeing ghostly apparitions and hearing strange noises near the Battery.

The USS Yorktown (Mount Pleasant) - The USS Yorktown is a retired aircraft carrier that is said to be haunted by the ghosts of former sailors who died on board. Visitors have reported seeing ghostly figures and experiencing strange occurrences on the ship.

St. James-Santee Episcopal Church (McClellanville) - St. James-Santee Episcopal Church is said to be haunted by the ghost of a former rector who died in the church. Visitors have reported seeing his ghostly figure and feeling his presence in the church.

The Dock Street Theatre (Charleston) - As mentioned before, the Dock Street Theatre is said to be haunted by the ghost of a former actor. Visitors have reported seeing his ghostly figure on stage and hearing strange noises in the building.

The Unitarian Church Cemetery (Charleston) - The Unitarian Church Cemetery is said to be haunted by the ghosts of former residents and soldiers who were buried there. Visitors have reported seeing ghostly apparitions and experiencing strange sensations while walking through the cemetery.

The Old Sheldon Church Ruins (Yemassee) - The Old Sheldon Church Ruins are the remains of a historic church that was burned during the Revolutionary War. Visitors have reported seeing ghostly apparitions and experiencing strange occurrences near the ruins.

The Ghost of Emily Geiger

The story of Emily Geiger is a well-known ghost story from the Lowcountry of South Carolina. Emily was a young messenger for the Patriots during the Revolutionary War, and her bravery and sacrifice have become the stuff of legend.

According to the story, Emily was tasked with delivering a message from General Nathanael Greene to General Thomas Sumter, who was leading a Patriot force in the area. Emily disguised herself as a young man and set out on horseback to deliver the message. Along the way, she was stopped by a group of British soldiers who became suspicious of her.

Knowing that the message she carried was vital to the Patriot cause, Emily swallowed the message, hoping to keep it from falling into British hands. She was later able to retrieve the message and deliver it to General Sumter, helping to secure a victory for the Patriots.

Today, Emily is said to haunt the area where she was stopped by the British soldiers. Visitors to the site have reported seeing a ghostly figure on horseback, believed to be Emily, riding through the area. Some have also reported hearing the sound of hooves and even seeing a spectral message being delivered.

The story of Emily Geiger has become an important part of the Lowcountry's history and folklore. Her bravery and sacrifice continue to inspire generations of South

Carolinians. Whether or not you believe in ghosts, the story of Emily Geiger is a testament to the courage and dedication of those who fought for freedom and independence during the Revolutionary War.

The Ghost of Anne Bonny

Anne Bonny was a notorious female pirate who lived during the 18th century and roamed the seas off the coast of Charleston and the surrounding Lowcountry. Her story is a fascinating one, full of adventure and intrigue, and her ghost is said to still haunt the area today.

According to legend, Anne Bonny was born in Ireland but spent much of her life in the Lowcountry of South Carolina. She was known for her fierce spirit and her love of adventure, and she joined forces with other pirates to plunder and pillage ships off the coast of Charleston.

Anne's story took a tragic turn when she was captured and sentenced to death for piracy. However, some say that her ghost still haunts the area, seeking revenge for her unjust fate.

Anne's ghost is said to appear near the site of her execution, now known as Execution Dock, located near White Point Garden in Charleston. Visitors to the area have reported seeing her ghostly figure, dressed in pirate attire and wielding a sword.

In addition to her ghostly presence, Anne's legacy has left an indelible mark on Charleston's history and culture. Her spirit of adventure and her fearless nature continue to inspire and intrigue visitors to the area, and her legend has become an important part of the Lowcountry's folklore.

The Gray Man of Isle of Palms

The Gray Man of Isle of Palms is a legendary ghost story that has been passed down for generations in the Lowcountry of South Carolina. The story goes that the ghost of a tall man dressed in gray and a wide brimmed hat appears on the beach of the Isle of Palms just before a hurricane or large storm is about to hit the coast.

According to the legend, the Gray Man is the ghost of a young man who drowned in the 1800s while trying to reach his fiancée during a storm. The story goes that the Gray Man appears to warn residents and visitors of the impending storm and to urge them to evacuate the area.

There are many reported sightings of the Gray Man prior to Hurricane Hugo in 1989 and again before Hurricane Florence in 2018. The most recent sightings were reported before Hurricane Dorian in 2019. However, there are also reports of the Gray Man appearing on calm, clear days, especially during the summer months.

Those who have claimed to have seen the Gray Man say that he is a benevolent spirit who only appears to help and protect those who live and vacation on the Isle of Palms. Many believe that if you see the Gray Man, your home and loved ones will be protected during the storm.

The Ghost of Alice Flagg

Alice Flagg is a well-known ghost from the Lowcountry of South Carolina, known for haunting the area around Murrells Inlet and the nearby Huntington Beach State Park. Her story is a tragic one, full of heartbreak and mystery, and her ghostly presence continues to intrigue and fascinate visitors to the area.

Alice was born in the mid-1800s to a prominent family in the Lowcountry. She fell in love with a man who her family did not approve of, and they forbade her from seeing him. Despite their objections, Alice continued to meet with her lover in secret, until her family discovered their relationship and forced him to leave.

Heartbroken, Alice became ill and died shortly thereafter. Her family buried her in a nearby cemetery, but her ghost is said to still haunt the area today.

According to legend, Alice's ghost can be seen wandering the beach at Huntington Beach State Park, dressed in a white gown and carrying a bouquet of flowers. Visitors to the area have reported seeing her ghostly figure and experiencing strange occurrences, such as the sudden appearance of flowers or the sound of a woman crying.

Alice's tragic story and her ghostly presence have become an important part of the Lowcountry's folklore, and her legend continues to captivate and intrigue visitors to the area. Whether or not you believe in ghosts, the story of Alice Flagg is a poignant reminder of the power of love and the pain of heartbreak, and her memory continues to live on in the hearts and minds of those who visit the Lowcountry.

The Haunting of Lands End Road

Lands End Road is a scenic drive that runs through the marshes and waterways of Hilton Head Island, South Carolina. The road is known for its natural beauty, but it is also famous for its haunting legends and ghostly presence.

According to legend, Lands End Road was once the site of a plantation owned by a wealthy family. The family had a daughter who fell in love with a slave, and when her father found out about their relationship, he forbade them from seeing each other.

The daughter was heartbroken and eventually died of a broken heart. Her ghost is said to still haunt the area, searching for her lost love.

Visitors to Lands End Road have reported seeing the ghostly figure of a young woman, dressed in a white gown and wandering the marshes. Some have also reported hearing strange noises and experiencing strange occurrences, such as car troubles or sudden drops in temperature.

In addition to the haunting of the plantation daughter, Lands End Road is also said to be haunted by the ghosts of slaves who were once forced to work on the plantation. Their ghostly presence is said to be felt throughout the area, with some visitors reporting feeling a sense of sadness or despair.

Despite the haunting legends and ghostly presence, Lands End Road remains a popular destination for tourists and locals alike. Whether you believe in ghosts or not, the haunting tales of Lands End Road are a testament to the area's rich history and cultural heritage. They continue to captivate and intrigue visitors.

Famous Lowcountry Cemeteries

Magnolia Cemetery - Located in Charleston, Magnolia Cemetery is one of the oldest cemeteries in the city, dating back to 1850. It is known for its beautiful gardens and stunning views of the Ashley River.

St. Helena's Episcopal Church Cemetery - Located on St. Helena Island, this cemetery is the final resting place of some of the area's most prominent African American families, including members of the Gullah Geechee community.

Beaufort National Cemetery - This cemetery is located in Beaufort and serves as the final resting place for thousands of veterans and their families.

Old Sheldon Church Ruins Cemetery - This cemetery is located in Yemassee and is the site of the ruins of the historic Old Sheldon Church. It is known for its stunning architecture and historic significance.

Beth Israel Cemetery - Located in Charleston, this cemetery is the final resting place for many members of the city's Jewish community. It is known for its beautiful gravestones and stunning views of the city.

St. James Goose Creek Episcopal Church Cemetery - Located in Goose Creek, this cemetery dates back to the 1700s and is the final resting place for many of the area's earliest settlers.

St. Andrew's Church Cemetery - Located in Mount Pleasant, this cemetery is the final resting place for many of the area's most prominent residents, including several governors of South Carolina.

St. Mary's Roman Catholic Cemetery - Located in Charleston, this cemetery is the final resting place for many of the area's Catholic residents. It is known for its beautiful statuary and stunning architecture.

Zion Cemetery and Baynard Mausoleum - Located in Hilton Head Island, this cemetery is the final resting place for many of the island's earliest residents. It is known for its beautiful mausoleum and stunning views of the surrounding area.

Christ Church Cemetery - Located in Mount Pleasant, this cemetery is the final resting place of many of the area's earliest settlers, including members of the influential Pinckney family.

Live Oak Cemetery - Located in Walterboro, this cemetery is known for its stunning oak trees, some of which are over 1,000 years old. It is the final resting place for many of the area's earliest settlers.

Bethany Cemetery - Located in Summerville, this cemetery is the final resting place for many of the area's early German settlers. It is known for its beautiful markers and stunning views of the surrounding countryside.

Bonneau Cemetery - Located in Bonneau, this cemetery is the final resting place for many of the area's earliest settlers. It is known for its historic significance and beautiful markers.

Holy Cross Cemetery - Located in Charleston, this cemetery is the final resting place for many of the area's Catholic residents. It is known for its beautiful markers and stunning views of the city.

Greenlawn Cemetery - Located in Beaufort, this cemetery is the final resting place for many of the area's earliest settlers.

It is known for its beautiful markers and stunning views of the Beaufort River.

Laurel Hill Cemetery - Located in Georgetown, this cemetery is the final resting place for many of the area's earliest settlers. It is known for its historic significance and stunning views of the surrounding marshes.

Animal Spirits

Some ghost stories from the Lowcountry of South Carolina involve ghost animals. Here are a few examples:

Hairy Houdini - This ghostly creature is said to haunt the marshes around Folly Island, just outside of Charleston. Legend has it that Hairy Houdini is a giant, ghostly boar that roams the area at night, causing mischief and scaring anyone who crosses his path.

Alice Ravenel Huger Smith's ghost cats- Alice Ravenel Huger Smith was a prominent artist and writer from Charleston, known for her depictions of the Lowcountry's natural beauty. She was also an avid animal lover, and it is said that the ghosts of her beloved cats still haunt her former home, now the Gibbes Museum of Art in downtown Charleston.

Ghost horses at the Old Village - The Old Village is a historic district in Mount Pleasant, just across the Cooper River from Charleston. Legend has it that the ghosts of horses can be seen trotting down the streets of the Old Village at night, a reminder of the area's equestrian past.

The Ghost Deer of Edisto Island - Legend has it that a ghostly deer haunts the woods around Edisto Island, just south of Charleston. The deer is said to be white and glowing, and it appears to visitors as a warning of impending danger or bad weather.

Ghost Dogs of Charleston - There are several stories of ghostly dogs that haunt the streets of Charleston at night. Some say that these ghostly dogs are the spirits of loyal pets that have passed away, while others believe that they are protectors of the city, keeping watch over its residents and visitors.

Ghost Cat of the Old Jail - The Old Jail is a historic building in Charleston that was used as a jail for over 100 years. Legend has it that the ghost of a cat haunts the building, meowing and scratching at the walls. Some believe that the cat is the spirit of a pet that belonged to one of the inmates, while others think that it is a guardian spirit protecting the building.

The Ghost of Drayton Hall - Drayton Hall is a historic plantation located just outside of Charleston. Legend has it that the ghost of a white stallion haunts the grounds, galloping through the woods at night. Some say that the ghostly horse is the spirit of one of the Drayton family's beloved horses, while others think that it is a symbol of the area's equestrian heritage.

While these stories are just legends and are not supported by any scientific evidence, they are an important part of the Lowcountry's folklore and cultural heritage, and they continue to intrigue and fascinate visitors to the area.

CHAPTER 6 LOWCOUNTRY CUISINE: A TASTE OF SOUTHERN TRADITION

The Lowcountry of South Carolina is known for its unique and delicious cuisine, which blends elements of Southern, African, and Caribbean cooking.

Traditional Dishes

Shrimp and Grits - Perhaps the most famous dish of the Lowcountry, shrimp and grits is a savory and filling meal made with fresh shrimp, stone-ground grits, and a variety of seasonings and sauces.

She-Crab Soup - This rich and creamy soup is made with crabmeat, cream, sherry, and roe from female blue crabs, which gives it a distinctive flavor and color.

Frogmore Stew - Also known as Lowcountry boil or Beaufort Stew, this one-pot dish features a variety of seafood, including shrimp, crab, and clams, as well as corn, potatoes, and sausage.

Hoppin' John - This traditional dish is made with black-eyed peas, rice, and pork, and is often served on New Year's Day as a symbol of good luck and prosperity.

Red Rice - A flavorful side dish made with rice, tomatoes, and spices. Red rice is a staple of Lowcountry cooking.

Oyster Roast - A Lowcountry tradition, oyster roasts are

outdoor parties where guests gather around a fire pit to roast oysters and enjoy each other's company.

Fried Chicken - A Southern classic, often served with sides like collard greens, mac and cheese, and sweet potato pie.

Barbecue - A Southern staple, with variations across the region. In the Lowcountry, barbecue is often made with a mustard-based sauce.

Okra Soup - A hearty soup made with okra, tomatoes, and sausage or chicken, often served with rice.

Seafood

The Lowcountry of South Carolina is known for its abundant and delicious seafood. Here are some of the most popular types of seafood that you can catch yourself or enjoy fresh in the Lowcountry.:

Shrimp: Shrimp is a staple of Lowcountry cuisine, and it's no wonder why - the waters around Charleston are home to some of the tastiest shrimp in the world.

Blue Crab: Blue crab is another popular seafood in the Lowcountry, with sweet and tender meat that is often used in crab cakes, gumbo, and other dishes.

Oysters: The Lowcountry is also famous for its oysters, which are harvested from the local marshes and bays and are often enjoyed raw or steamed.

Redfish: Redfish, also known as red drum, is a popular game fish in the Lowcountry that is prized for its mild and flaky meat.

Flounder: Flounder is another popular game fish in the Lowcountry, with delicate white meat that is often pan-fried or baked.

Grouper: Grouper is a large saltwater fish that is often caught offshore and is prized for its firm and flavorful meat.

Sheepshead: Sheepshead is a smaller saltwater fish that is often caught around pilings and similar structures. It is known for its white and flaky meat.

Clams: Clams are another popular seafood in the Lowcountry, with a sweet and briny flavor that is often used in stews and chowders.

Mahi-mahi: Mahi-mahi, also known as dolphin fish, is a large and colorful saltwater fish that is prized for its firm and flavorful meat.

These are just a few of the many types of seafood that you can catch and enjoy in the Lowcountry of South Carolina. Whether you're an angler or just a seafood lover, the Lowcountry offers a bounty of delicious options.

Beverages

These beverages are an important part of the Lowcountry's culinary and social traditions, and are often enjoyed at family gatherings, outdoor events, and other social occasions.

Sweet Tea - A refreshing and sweetened iced tea, often served with a slice of lemon.

Lemonade - Freshly squeezed lemonade is a popular summer drink in the Lowcountry.

Mint Julep - A classic cocktail made with bourbon, mint, sugar, and water, and often served at horse races and other social events.

Tea Punch - A fruity, refreshing punch made with black tea, pineapple juice, and lemon juice.

Palmetto Beer - A local beer brewed in Charleston, known for its smooth, balanced flavor.

Firefly Sweet Tea Vodka - A popular Lowcountry spirit made with sweet tea and vodka, often mixed with lemonade for a refreshing summer cocktail.

Charleston Sipper - A refreshing cocktail made with gin, grapefruit juice, and honey syrup, often garnished with a sprig of rosemary.

Sweet Tea

Sweet tea is a staple of Southern cuisine and a beloved beverage throughout the Lowcountry of South Carolina. While the exact origins of sweet tea are unclear, it is widely believed to have originated in the South in the 19th century, when iced tea became popular as a refreshing summer drink.

The town of Summerville, South Carolina, is known as the birthplace of sweet tea. According to legend, in 1890, a local tea plantation owner named Dr. Charles Shephard hosted a party for guests who were used to drinking hot tea. When the temperature soared, he added ice to the tea and served it cold. To make the tea more palatable, he added sugar, which resulted in a delicious and refreshing beverage that his guests loved. Thus, sweet tea was born.

Summerville has since become known as "The Birthplace of Sweet Tea," and the town celebrates this heritage with an annual Sweet Tea Festival, which features tastings, live music, and other activities. Sweet tea remains a beloved beverage throughout the South and is often served with meals, at social gatherings, and during hot summer afternoons.

Today, sweet tea is a cultural icon of the South and an important part of the Lowcountry's culinary heritage. Whether enjoyed on a front porch on a hot summer day or paired with a savory meal, sweet tea continues to be a symbol of hospitality, community, and Southern tradition.

Sweets and Treats

BENNE WAFERS

Benne wafers are a traditional Southern snack that originated in the Lowcountry of South Carolina. They are thin and crispy cookies made with sesame seeds, sugar, and butter, and are often enjoyed as a sweet and nutty treat.

The name "benne" comes from the Bantu word for sesame seeds, which were brought to the United States by West African slaves. The seeds were then incorporated into traditional Southern cuisine, and eventually became a key ingredient in the beloved benne wafer.

To make benne wafers, sesame seeds are toasted and then combined with butter, sugar, flour, and sometimes a small amount of salt. The dough is then rolled out and cut into thin circles, which are baked until they are golden brown and crispy.

Benne wafers are a popular snack throughout the South, and are often served at parties, picnics, and other gatherings. They are also sold at local markets and specialty food stores. They are a classic Southern treat that has been enjoyed for generations.

CHARLESTON CHEWS

Charleston Chews are a traditional Southern dessert that originated in Charleston, South Carolina. They are sweet and chewy treats made with pecans, coconut, and caramel, and are often sold at local bakeries and candy shops.

To make Charleston Chews, pecans and coconut are mixed together and then coated in a sweet and gooey caramel sauce. The mixture is then poured into a baking dish and baked until it is firm and chewy. Once cooled, the mixture is cut into small squares or rectangles and served as a delicious and indulgent dessert.

They are then often packaged in small bags or boxes, making them a popular souvenir for visitors to Charleston looking to take a taste of the city's culinary heritage home with them.

CHEESE STRAWS

Cheese straws are a traditional Southern snack that are popular in the Lowcountry of South Carolina. They are crispy and crunchy cheese-flavored sticks made with flour, butter, and cheese, and are often served as an appetizer or snack.

To make cheese straws, flour, butter, and cheese are mixed together to create a dough that is then rolled out and cut into thin sticks. The sticks are then baked in the oven until they are crispy and golden brown, resulting in a delicious and savory snack that is perfect for any occasion.

Cheese straws are a beloved snack in the South, and they are often served at parties, picnics, and other gatherings. They can be made with a variety of different cheeses, such as cheddar, parmesan, or pecorino romano, and can be seasoned with spices such as cayenne pepper or black pepper for an extra kick of flavor.

GROUNDNUT CAKE

Groundnut cake is a traditional Southern dessert that is believed to have originated in the Lowcountry of South Carolina. It is made with a combination of ground peanuts, sugar, and flour, and has a rich and nutty flavor. It's more of a cookie than a cake.

To make groundnut cake, peanuts are ground into a fine powder and combined with flour, sugar, and other ingredients such as baking powder, cinnamon, and nutmeg. The mixture is then baked in the oven until it is golden brown and cooked through. They are lacey and crisp.

Groundnut cake is a delicious and unique dessert that is an important part of the culinary heritage of the Lowcountry of

South Carolina. It is a testament to the ingenuity and creativity of Southern cooks, who have found ways to use local ingredients to create delicious and satisfying dishes.

HUGUENOT TORTE

Huguenot Torte is a traditional Southern dessert that originated in Charleston, South Carolina. It is a rich and nutty cake made with apples. Don't let the name fool you. There's no crust in this dessert.

To make Huguenot Torte, toasted pecans and apples are mixed into a sweet thick batter. The batter is then poured into a cake pan and baked until it is golden brown and cooked through. The resulting cake is dense and moist, with a sweet and nutty flavor.

LADY BALTIMORE CAKE

Lady Baltimore cake is a traditional Southern cake that is believed to have originated in Charleston, in the early 20th century by a resident named Alicia Rhett Mayberry. It is a layered cake that consists of light and airy sponge cake layers, filled with a sweet and fluffy filling made with dried fruits, nuts, and coconut, and then frosted with a boiled frosting.

The filling for Lady Baltimore cake typically includes dried figs, raisins, and candied cherries, along with chopped nuts such as pecans or almonds. The filling is typically cooked together with sugar, water, and sometimes a small amount of liqueur to create a sweet and fruity mixture that is then spread between the cake layers.

The frosting for Lady Baltimore cake is made by boiling sugar and water together to create a syrup, which is then beaten with egg whites and sometimes vanilla extract until it becomes light and fluffy. The frosting is then spread over the top and sides of the cake to create a smooth and creamy finish. Its light and delicate flavor make it a perfect dessert for warm weather, and its beautiful appearance makes it a stunning centerpiece for any dessert table.

The Lowcountry of South Carolina is known for its rich culinary heritage, unique ingredients, and delicious cuisine. From fresh seafood to Gullah Geechee vegetables, the region offers a variety of flavors and dishes that reflect the area's history and culture. Sweet tea, a classic Southern beverage that originated in the Lowcountry, is a beloved staple that perfectly complements the region's flavorful dishes. Whether you're savoring a bowl of shrimp and grits, snacking on cheese straws, or indulging in a slice of Huguenot torte, the food and sweet tea of the Lowcountry are sure to leave a lasting impression on your taste buds.

The Oldest Restaurants & Bars

The Lowcountry of South Carolina is home to a few restaurants and bars that have been in business for over a century. Here are some of the oldest restaurants in the area and what they are known for:

The Old Post Office Restaurant - Edisto Island: The Old Post Office Restaurant has been in business for over 100 years and is known for its Southern-style cuisine, particularly its fried chicken, shrimp and grits, and crab cakes.

Hyman's Seafood - Charleston: Hyman's Seafood has been in business for over 125 years and is known for its fresh seafood, particularly its fried seafood platters and shrimp and grits.

The Blind Tiger - Charleston: The Blind Tiger has been in business since 1803 and is known for its historic atmosphere, as well as its cocktails and live music.

The Palace Hotel - Charleston: The Palace Hotel has been in business since 1890 and is known for its historic atmosphere and strong drinks.

The Oldest Liquor Store in the United States

The Tavern At Rainbow Row has been in continuous operation since 1686. All this time they have sold liquor and spirits to Charlestonians. They became a barber shop during Prohibition, but you could still buy booze in the backroom. Today you can stop in and buy a bottle of whatever you fancy. The store still has the original hardwood floors and brick walls.

CHAPTER 7: THE NATURAL TREASURES OF THE LOWCOUNTRY: A JOURNEY THROUGH ITS LANDSCAPES AND WILDLIFE

The Lowcountry of South Carolina is a region of incredible natural beauty, with a landscape that includes salt marshes, tidal creeks, oak forests, and sandy beaches. One of the most unique features of the Lowcountry is its extensive system of tidal creeks and rivers, which wind their way through the marshes and provide a vital habitat for a diverse range of wildlife.

The salt marshes of the Lowcountry are also a unique and important ecosystem, providing a nursery and feeding ground for many species of fish, crabs, and shellfish. These marshes are also home to a variety of birds, including egrets, herons, and ospreys, which can often be seen wading through the shallow waters in search of food.

In addition to the marshes, the Lowcountry is also home to a number of other unique natural features, such as the Angel Oak, a massive live oak tree that is estimated to be over 400 years old and is one of the largest of its kind in the world. The Lowcountry is also home to several species of carnivorous plants, such as the Venus flytrap and the pitcher plant, which thrive in the area's moist, nutrient-poor soils.

The Lowcountry's beaches are another major draw for visitors, with miles of unspoiled coastline offering opportunities for swimming, sunbathing, and beachcombing. Several of these beaches, such as Folly Beach and Isle of

Palms, are also popular surfing spots.

Overall, the natural beauty of the Lowcountry of South Carolina is a major part of what makes the area so special. From the salt marshes to the beaches, the region is a haven for wildlife and a source of endless wonder and inspiration for visitors and residents alike.

Outdoor Activities

There are a variety of outdoor activities and adventures that visitors can enjoy in Charleston, SC and the surrounding Lowcountry areas. Here are some examples:

Explore the beaches: The Charleston area is home to a number of beautiful beaches, including Folly Beach, Sullivan's Island, and Isle of Palms. Visitors can swim, sunbathe, surf, or simply relax and take in the stunning ocean views.

Go kayaking or paddleboarding: The Lowcountry is full of waterways, including rivers, creeks, and marshes, which make for great kayaking and paddleboarding adventures. Companies like Charleston Outdoor Adventures offer guided tours and rentals for those who want to explore the area's natural beauty from the water.

Take a bike tour: Biking is a great way to explore the historic streets of Charleston and get some exercise at the same time. There are several bike tour companies in the city that offer guided tours of the city's historic landmarks and neighborhoods.

Visit a state park: The Charleston area is home to several

state parks, including James Island County Park and Hunting Island State Park. Visitors can hike, bike, swim, and enjoy a variety of outdoor activities in these beautiful natural settings.

Go fishing: With its proximity to the ocean, rivers, and marshes, the Lowcountry is a great place to go fishing. Visitors can try their luck at catching a variety of fish, including redfish, trout, and flounder.

Play golf: The Charleston area is home to several world-class golf courses, including Kiawah Island Golf Resort and Wild Dunes Resort. Golf enthusiasts can enjoy a round of golf while taking in the beautiful Lowcountry scenery.

Beaches

The Lowcountry of South Carolina is home to several beautiful beaches that offer a variety of activities and attractions. Here are some of the most popular beaches in the area and what they are known for:

Folly Beach: Located just outside of Charleston, Folly Beach is known for its laid-back vibe and vibrant surf culture. It's a popular spot for surfing, kayaking, and paddleboarding, and also offers great fishing and birdwatching opportunities.

Isle of Palms: This barrier island is located just north of Charleston and is known for its pristine beaches, upscale resorts, and championship golf courses. It's a popular spot for families and couples looking for a relaxing beach vacation.

Kiawah Island: This barrier island is located just south of

Charleston and is known for its luxury resorts, world-class golf courses, and stunning natural beauty. Visitors can enjoy a variety of activities, including swimming, kayaking, fishing, and cycling.

Edisto Beach: Located about an hour south of Charleston, Edisto Beach is a quiet and secluded spot that's perfect for those looking to escape the crowds. It's known for its pristine beaches, beautiful sunsets, and excellent shelling opportunities.

Hunting Island State Park: Located about 90 minutes south of Charleston, Hunting Island State Park is home to a beautiful beach, as well as hiking trails, camping sites, and a historic lighthouse. It's a popular spot for fishing, birdwatching, and exploring the park's unique maritime forest.

Kayaking & Paddleboarding

The Lowcountry is home to a variety of waterways, including rivers, creeks, and marshes, which make for great kayaking and paddleboarding adventures. Here are some popular spots to go kayaking or paddleboarding and what you can see while you're there:

Shem Creek: Located in Mount Pleasant, Shem Creek is a popular spot for kayaking and paddleboarding. You can paddle past shrimp boats, fishing docks, and waterfront restaurants, and catch a glimpse of local wildlife like pelicans and dolphins.

Folly River: The Folly River is a great spot for kayaking and paddleboarding, with calm waters and beautiful scenery. You can paddle past marshes, oyster beds, and small islands, and may even see dolphins swimming nearby.

Kiawah River: The Kiawah River is a scenic spot for kayaking or paddleboarding, with calm waters and beautiful views of the Lowcountry landscape. You may see osprey and other bird species, as well as dolphins and other marine life.

Wando River: The Wando River is a popular spot for kayaking and paddleboarding, with easy access from Mount Pleasant. You can paddle past marshes and wildlife areas, and may see bald eagles, osprey, and other bird species.

Francis Marion National Forest: The Francis Marion National Forest is a vast wilderness area that offers a variety of kayaking and paddleboarding opportunities. You can explore the forest's many creeks and waterways, and see a variety of wildlife, including alligators, otters, and various bird species.

Cypress Gardens: Located in Moncks Corner, Cypress Gardens is a popular spot for kayaking or paddleboarding in a beautiful natural setting. You can paddle through cypress trees, Spanish moss, and other unique scenery, and may see turtles, snakes, and various bird species.

Ashley River: The Ashley River is a beautiful spot for kayaking or paddleboarding, with views of historic plantations and other landmarks. You can paddle past marshes, forests, and even see dolphins in the river.

Charleston Harbor: The Charleston Harbor is a popular spot for kayaking or paddleboarding, with views of the city skyline and the historic forts and lighthouses that dot the harbor. You may also see ships and other boats passing by.

Beaufort Waterfront Park: Located in Beaufort, the Beaufort Waterfront Park is a scenic spot for kayaking or paddleboarding, with views of the historic downtown area and the nearby marshes. You can paddle through the Intracoastal Waterway and may see dolphins and other marine life.

These are just a few examples of the many places to go kayaking or paddleboarding in the Lowcountry of South Carolina. Each spot offers its own unique scenery and wildlife, making it a great way to explore the area's natural beauty.

Biking

Charleston and the surrounding areas offer a variety of scenic and enjoyable bike paths and routes for cyclists of all levels. Here are some of the best places to ride your bike in Charleston and the Lowcountry:

The Ravenel Bridge: The Ravenel Bridge is a popular spot for cycling, with a dedicated bike lane that provides stunning views of Charleston Harbor.

The West Ashley Greenway: The West Ashley Greenway is a 10.5-mile paved trail that runs through West Ashley and offers a scenic ride through parks and marshes.

The James Island County Park: The James Island County Park offers a 10-mile paved trail through a beautiful wooded area, as well as access to other bike paths and trails in the park.

The Wando Riverfront Park: The Wando Riverfront Park

offers a 1.5-mile paved trail with beautiful views of the Wando River and nearby marshes.

The Palmetto Trail: The Palmetto Trail is a statewide network of trails that includes several sections in the Lowcountry, offering a mix of paved and unpaved paths through forests, swamps, and other natural areas.

The Kiawah Island Parkway: The Kiawah Island Parkway offers a scenic ride through the beautiful and exclusive Kiawah Island, with views of the beach, marshes, and forests.

The Ashley River Historic District: The Ashley River Historic District offers a 10-mile loop through some of Charleston's oldest and most historic neighborhoods, with plenty of beautiful homes and gardens to admire along the way.

The North Charleston and Summerville Trail System: The North Charleston and Summerville Trail System is a network of trails that includes both paved and unpaved paths, with a total length of over 22 miles.

The Mount Pleasant Waterfront Park: The Mount Pleasant Waterfront Park offers a scenic ride along the Cooper River, with stunning views of downtown Charleston and the Ravenel Bridge.

The Edisto Island National Scenic Byway: The Edisto Island National Scenic Byway offers a 16-mile bike route through some of the Lowcountry's most beautiful natural areas, including marshes, forests, and beaches.

The Fort Moultrie Loop: The Fort Moultrie Loop is a 7-mile ride on Sullivan's Island that takes you past historic sites, beautiful beaches, and scenic marshes.

These routes offer a mix of natural beauty and historic charm and are great options for cyclists of all levels.

Wildlife

The Lowcountry of South Carolina is home to a diverse range of wildlife, including:

Alligators: One of the most iconic animals in the Lowcountry, alligators can be found in freshwater marshes, rivers, and ponds throughout the area.

Dolphins: The waters around Charleston are home to several pods of Atlantic bottlenose dolphins, which can often be seen swimming and playing in the harbor and along the coast.

Sea turtles: Several species of sea turtles nest on the beaches of the Lowcountry, including loggerheads, green turtles, and leatherbacks.

Bald eagles: These majestic birds of prey can often be seen soaring over marshes and waterways in search of fish and other prey.

Bobcats: These elusive wildcats can be found throughout the Lowcountry, living in dense forests and wetlands.

Red foxes: These small, bushy-tailed canids are common in the Lowcountry and can be seen hunting for prey in open fields and wooded areas.

White-tailed deer: These graceful animals can be found in wooded areas throughout the Lowcountry, often seen grazing in fields and along the edges of forests.

Wild turkeys: These large birds are common in the

Lowcountry and can often be seen foraging for food in open fields and wooded areas.

Red-tailed hawks: These birds of prey are commonly seen soaring over open fields and wetlands, hunting for rodents and other small animals.

River otters: These playful animals can be found in rivers, lakes, and marshes throughout the Lowcountry, often seen swimming and playing in the water.

These are just a few examples of the many different species of wildlife that call the Lowcountry of South Carolina home. Visitors to the area can experience these animals and more through wildlife tours, hiking trails, and other outdoor activities.

The Angel Oak

The Angel Oak is a massive live oak tree located on Johns Island, just outside of Charleston, South Carolina. It is estimated to be between 400 and 500 years old and stands 66.5 feet tall. Its trunk circumference of 28 feet. Its canopy covers an area of about 17,000 square feet, making it one of the largest live oak trees in the world.

The tree is named after Justus Angel and his wife Martha Waight Angel, who owned the land on which the tree now stands in the late 18th century. The property was later sold and passed through several owners before being acquired by the City of Charleston in 1991.

The Angel Oak has become a popular tourist attraction and is visited by thousands of people each year. The tree has been featured in several movies and TV shows, including the movie "The Patriot" and the TV series "Army Wives." It has also been the subject of many paintings, photographs, and other works of art.

Despite its age, the Angel Oak is still growing and producing acorns. The tree is also home to a variety of wildlife, including squirrels, birds, and insects. The City of Charleston has taken steps to protect and preserve the tree, including limiting development in the surrounding area and providing support for the tree's massive branches.

The Southeastern Wildlife Exposition

The Southeastern Wildlife Exposition, also known as SEWE, is an annual three-day celebration of wildlife and nature that takes place in Charleston, South Carolina. The event showcases the work of artists, sculptors, and carvers, as well as the talents of wildlife experts, conservationists, and educators. Visitors to the Southeastern Wildlife Exposition can enjoy a wide range of activities, such as wildlife presentations, bird of prey demonstrations, hunting and fishing seminars, and retriever and pointer trials. SEWE also features an art show and sale, a marketplace, and a variety of food and beverage options. The Southeastern Wildlife Exposition is considered one of the premier wildlife events in the country and attracts visitors from all over the world.

SEWE was founded in 1983 by a group of Charleston businessmen and wildlife enthusiasts.

The event takes place annually in mid-February and typically attracts more than 40,000 visitors over the course of three days.

SEWE is a nonprofit organization that aims to promote wildlife and nature conservation, education, and appreciation.

The event features more than 500 artists and exhibitors from around the world, showcasing everything from paintings and sculptures to jewelry and clothing.

SEWE offers a variety of educational and interactive experiences, including live animal exhibits, bird of prey demonstrations, and fly-fishing demonstrations.

The event also includes several competitions, such as the Southeastern Wildlife Exposition Retriever Trials, the DockDogs World Qualifying Championships, and the Southeastern Youth Wildlife Art Contest.

SEWE has an economic impact of more than $50 million on the Charleston area each year.

SEWE is one of the largest wildlife art and nature events in the country and has been recognized as one of the top 20 events in the Southeast by the Southeast Tourism Society.

Conservation

The Lowcountry has unique and diverse wildlife, including endangered and threatened species. As a result, there are several wildlife conservation efforts in and near Charleston, South Carolina.

Francis Marion National Forest: This forest is managed by the US Forest Service and spans over 250,000 acres. It is home to many species of wildlife, including the endangered red-cockaded woodpecker, and is managed for conservation purposes.

Cape Romain National Wildlife Refuge: Located near Charleston, this refuge covers over 64,000 acres and is managed by the US Fish and Wildlife Service. It is home to several endangered and threatened species, including the loggerhead sea turtle and the red wolf.

Sewee Visitor and Environmental Education Center: This educational center near Charleston is focused on promoting conservation and environmental awareness. It offers programs and events for all ages to learn about the natural environment and wildlife of the area.

South Carolina Aquarium: The aquarium, located in Charleston, features exhibits, and educational programs focused on the conservation of marine life and their habitats.

South Carolina Department of Natural Resources: The state agency is responsible for managing and conserving the wildlife resources of South Carolina. They offer education programs and initiatives to promote wildlife conservation and management.

Audubon South Carolina: This organization is dedicated to protecting birds and their habitats in South Carolina through education, advocacy, and conservation programs.

These efforts help to ensure that these resources are protected for future generations to enjoy and appreciate.

CHAPTER 8 SPORTS AND RECREATION

The Lowcountry offers many options for sports and recreation.

Boating

The Lowcountry is home to numerous marinas and yacht clubs, and the waterways offer plenty of opportunities for boaters of all kinds. Some of the boating events that take place in and near Charleston include the Charleston Race Week, the Charleston Harbor Fest, and the Charleston In-Water Boat Show. Additionally, there are plenty of fishing tournaments, sailing regattas, and paddle sports events throughout the year. The region is also home to a number of guided boat tours, sunset cruises, and eco-tours, giving visitors the opportunity to explore the unique waterways and wildlife of the Lowcountry.

Charleston Harbor Fest - This is a three-day festival held in April at the Charleston Harbor Resort & Marina. The festival includes live music, food and drinks, and events for children. Boating enthusiasts can also participate in the boat show, fishing tournaments, and sailing regattas.

Charleston In-Water Boat Show - This annual event takes place in April and is one of the largest boat shows in the Southeast. Held at the Charleston City Marina, visitors can see a wide range of boats, from luxury yachts to small sailboats.

Charleston Race Week - This is a four-day sailing event held in April. The regatta is open to sailors of all levels and includes races in the harbor and ocean. In addition to the races, there are also social events and parties.

Charleston Harbor Resort & Marina Billfish Tournament - This is an annual fishing tournament held in July. The tournament attracts fishermen from all over the country to compete for cash prizes and trophies.

Charleston Sailing Week - This annual event takes place in April and is hosted by the Charleston Yacht Club. The regatta features racing in the Charleston Harbor and offshore, and also includes social events and parties for participants.

Charleston Maritime Festival - This is a two-day event held in November at the Charleston Maritime Center. The festival includes educational exhibits, historic ship tours, and live music. Visitors can also see boats on display and participate in family-friendly activities.

Hilton Head Island Boat Show: This annual event is held in the spring at the Windmill Harbour Yacht Basin. It features the latest boats and marine products, along with seminars and entertainment.

HarbourFest: This summer-long celebration at Shelter Cove Harbour and Marina on Hilton Head Island features live music, fireworks, and family-friendly activities, including boat tours and water sports.

Beaufort Water Festival: This annual event in the summer features live music, a craft fair, and a variety of water-related activities, including boat races, a fishing tournament, and a river rally. It takes place in Beaufort, which is located about 40 miles from Hilton Head.

Fishing

Charleston and the surrounding areas offer excellent opportunities for both saltwater and freshwater fishing. Here are some of the best places to fish and what you can catch:

Charleston Harbor: Charleston Harbor is a great spot for saltwater fishing, with a variety of species including redfish, flounder, trout, and sheepshead.

Folly Beach Pier: The Folly Beach Pier is a popular spot for saltwater fishing, with catches including king mackerel, Spanish mackerel, and bluefish.

Isle of Palms Pier: The Isle of Palms Pier is another great spot for saltwater fishing, with catches including redfish, Spanish mackerel, and shark.

Santee Cooper Lakes: The Santee Cooper Lakes are a top freshwater fishing destination, with species including largemouth bass, catfish, and crappie.

Edisto Beach State Park: Edisto Beach State Park offers both saltwater and freshwater fishing, with catches including redfish, trout, and catfish.

Lake Moultrie: Lake Moultrie is another top freshwater fishing spot, with species including largemouth bass, catfish, and bream.

Johns Island County Park: Johns Island County Park offers freshwater fishing in a stocked pond, with catches including catfish, bream, and bass.

Wappoo Cut Boat Landing: Wappoo Cut Boat Landing is a popular spot for saltwater fishing, with catches including redfish, trout, and flounder.

Shem Creek Park: Shem Creek Park offers saltwater fishing with catches including redfish, trout, and flounder.

Cooper River: The Cooper River is a popular spot for saltwater fishing, with catches including redfish, shark, and sheepshead.

Kiawah Island: Kiawah Island offers saltwater fishing with catches including redfish, trout, and shark.

Stono River: The Stono River offers saltwater fishing with catches including redfish, trout, and flounder.

These are just a few of the many great fishing spots in the Charleston area. Whether you're a seasoned angler or just starting out, there's plenty of opportunities to catch a variety of fish in the Lowcountry.

Fishing Tournaments

There are several fishing tournaments held in the Lowcountry of South Carolina each year, including:

Charleston Harbor Billfish Tournament: This is an annual tournament held in June that attracts anglers from all over the world who come to catch billfish species like marlin and sailfish in the waters around Charleston.

Megadock Billfishing Tournament: This tournament is held in July and is also focused on billfish species like marlin and sailfish. The tournament is based out of the Charleston City

Marina and offers cash prizes for the biggest catches.

Edisto Billfish Invitational: This tournament is held in August and is focused on billfish like marlin and sailfish, as well as other game fish like tuna and wahoo. It is based out of the Edisto Marina on Edisto Island.

Lowcountry Redfish Cup: This is a series of tournaments held throughout the year that focuses on redfish, a popular game fish in the Lowcountry. Anglers compete for cash prizes in each tournament, and the series culminates in a championship event in the fall.

Lowcountry Kayak Anglers: This is a series of kayak fishing tournaments held throughout the year in the Lowcountry. Anglers fish from kayaks and compete for cash prizes in categories like biggest redfish, biggest flounder, and biggest trout.

Golf

Charleston, SC and the surrounding area are home to several world-renowned golf courses. Here are some of the most famous ones and what makes them so special:

Kiawah Island Golf Resort: Located just south of Charleston on Kiawah Island, this resort is home to five championship golf courses, including the famous Ocean Course. The Ocean Course has hosted several major championships, including the PGA Championship and the Ryder Cup, and is known for its challenging layout and stunning views of the Atlantic Ocean.

Harbour Town Golf Links: Located on Hilton Head Island,

Harbour Town Golf Links is home to the PGA Tour's RBC Heritage tournament. The course is known for its narrow fairways, small greens, and iconic lighthouse that serves as a backdrop to the 18th hole.

The Links at Wild Dunes: Located on the Isle of Palms just north of Charleston, this golf course is known for its scenic views of the Atlantic Ocean and its challenging layout that winds through sand dunes and coastal marshes.

Bulls Bay Golf Club: Located just north of Charleston in Awendaw, Bulls Bay Golf Club is known for its challenging layout that winds through oak and pine forests and features deep bunkers and water hazards.

Stono Ferry Golf Course: Located just south of Charleston on Johns Island, Stono Ferry Golf Course is known for its beautiful Lowcountry scenery and its challenging layout that features water hazards, sand bunkers, and tight fairways. The course is also home to the annual Charleston Classic golf tournament.

Oak Point Golf Course: Also located on Kiawah Island, Oak Point Golf Course is known for its challenging layout that features water hazards and marshes. The course is designed to challenge golfers of all skill levels and offers stunning views of the island's natural beauty.

Patriots Point Links: Located in Mount Pleasant just across the harbor from Charleston, Patriots Point Links offers stunning views of the Charleston skyline and is known for its challenging layout that winds through coastal marshes and wetlands.

Golfers from around the world come to the Lowcountry to

experience these challenging and beautiful courses that are steeped in history and tradition.

Tennis

The most prominent tennis tournament in Charleston, South Carolina is the Volvo Car Open, which is a professional women's tennis tournament that is part of the Women's Tennis Association (WTA) tour. The tournament takes place at the Family Circle Tennis Center on Daniel Island every year in early April and features some of the top female players in the world. The tournament is played on green clay courts, which are a unique feature compared to other WTA events. In addition to the Volvo Car Open, there are also several other amateur and junior tournaments that take place throughout the year at various tennis clubs and facilities in the Charleston area. The Lowcountry has several private and public tennis courts.

Family Circle Tennis Center - Home to the Volvo Car Open, this facility has 17 Har-Tru courts, including a 10,200-seat stadium court.

Charleston Tennis Center - This public facility has 13 Har-Tru courts, lights for night play, and offers clinics and lessons for all ages and skill levels.

LTP Tennis - Located in Mount Pleasant, this tennis club has 12 clay courts and offers lessons, clinics, and league play.

Wild Dunes Resort - This resort on Isle of Palms has 17 Har-Tru courts, including a stadium court, and offers lessons and clinics for resort guests and non-guests.

Roy Barth Tennis Center - Part of the Kiawah Island Golf Resort, this center has 12 Har-Tru courts and offers clinics, lessons, and league play.

Seabrook Island Racquet Club - This facility on Seabrook Island has 15 Har-Tru courts and offers clinics, lessons, and league play.

Daniel Island Club - This private club on Daniel Island has 10 Har-Tru courts, two grass courts, and two hard courts, as well as a stadium court and clubhouse. Membership is required to use the facilities.

Snee Farm Country Club - This private club in Mount Pleasant has nine Har-Tru courts and offers lessons and league play.

Amateur Sports

There are several amateur league sports teams that can be seen in Charleston, SC and the surrounding areas. Here are a few examples:

Charleston Battery - This is a professional soccer team that plays in the United Soccer League. They play their home games at Patriots Point Soccer Complex in nearby Mount Pleasant.

Charleston RiverDogs - This is a minor league baseball team that plays in the South Atlantic League. They play their home games at Joseph P. Riley Jr. Park in Charleston. The RiverDogs have been affiliated with Major League Baseball's

New York Yankees since their inception in 1994.

Charleston Rugby Club - This is a men's and women's rugby club that competes in the Carolinas Geographic Rugby Union. They play their home matches at different locations throughout the area.

Charleston Outlaws - This is a semi-professional football team that competes in the Gridiron Developmental Football League. They play their home games at Gethers Funeral Home Field in North Charleston.

Charleston Lacrosse Club - This is a men's lacrosse club that competes in the South Carolina Lacrosse League. They play their home games at different locations throughout the area.

There are also several other amateur and recreational sports leagues and teams in the Charleston area, including basketball, volleyball, flag football, and more.

Hilton Head Island Concours d'Elegance

The Hilton Head Island Concours d'Elegance is an annual automobile and motorcycle showcase held in Hilton Head Island, South Carolina. The event takes place over the course of a week and features a variety of activities, including car and motorcycle displays, vintage aircraft exhibits, and a charity auction.

The main event is a judged competition showcasing classic, antique, and high-performance cars and motorcycles from around the world. The event also includes lectures, symposiums, and other automotive-related activities.

The Hilton Head Island Concours d'Elegance is considered one of the premier automotive events in the Southeastern United States.

The Cooper River Bridge Run

The Cooper River Bridge Run is an annual 10-kilometer race that takes place in Charleston, South Carolina.

The race was first held in 1978 and has been held annually ever since, except for 2020 when it was cancelled due to the COVID-19 pandemic.

The course starts in Mount Pleasant, crosses the Arthur Ravenel Jr. Bridge over the Cooper River, and finishes in downtown Charleston.

The Arthur Ravenel Jr. Bridge, which opened in 2005, is the third longest cable-stayed bridge in the Western Hemisphere and the longest in North America.

The Cooper River Bridge Run is the third largest 10-kilometer race in the United States, with an average of over 30,000 participants each year.

The race has a significant economic impact on the Charleston area, with an estimated $30 million generated annually from hotel bookings, restaurant visits, and other tourism-related activities.

The Cooper River Bridge Run is known for its festive

atmosphere, with live music and entertainment along the course and a post-race party in downtown Charleston.

The event has also become a charitable fundraiser, with proceeds benefiting a variety of local organizations each year.

CHAPTER 9 LOWCOUNTRY ARTS AND ENTERTAINMENT: FROM GULLAH TRADITIONS TO WORLD-CLASS PERFORMANCES

The arts and entertainment scene in the Lowcountry is vibrant and diverse, featuring a wide variety of options for residents and visitors alike. The city is home to numerous theaters, galleries, and performance spaces, showcasing everything from classic plays and musicals to contemporary art and cutting-edge performances. There are also many cultural events and festivals throughout the year, including the Spoleto Festival USA, Charleston Wine + Food Festival, and the Charleston Fashion Week. Additionally, Charleston is known for its vibrant music scene, with numerous venues hosting live performances of everything from jazz and blues to rock and country. The city also has a strong literary tradition, with many writers and poets calling the area home, and there are numerous bookstores and literary events throughout the year.

Spoleto Festival USA

Spoleto Festival USA is an annual performing arts festival held in Charleston, South Carolina. The festival was founded in 1977 by composer Gian Carlo Menotti, who sought to create an American counterpart to the Festival of Two Worlds in Spoleto, Italy.

The festival features a variety of performances including

opera, theater, dance, music, and visual arts. Spoleto Festival USA has become one of the leading festivals of its kind in the country and attracts thousands of visitors each year.

The festival runs for 17 days and features both established and emerging artists from around the world.

Many famous performers have participated in the Spoleto Festival USA throughout its history. Some notable performers have included renowned opera singer Renée Fleming, acclaimed jazz musician Wynton Marsalis, and legendary cellist Yo-Yo Ma.

Other famous performers have included contemporary composers Philip Glass and John Adams, as well as dance troupes such as the Alvin Ailey American Dance Theater.

Charleston Wine + Food Festival

The Charleston Wine + Food Festival is an annual five-day event held in Charleston, South Carolina that celebrates the best of Southern cuisine, spirits, and hospitality.

The festival features over 100 unique culinary experiences, including chef demonstrations, wine tastings, cooking classes, and exclusive dinners hosted by renowned chefs.

It showcases the Lowcountry's rich culinary heritage and the innovative techniques and flavors of its modern food scene. In addition to its focus on food and drink, the festival also includes live music performances, art exhibitions, and other cultural events.

The festival attracts food lovers, wine enthusiasts, and

industry professionals from around the world.

Many famous chefs and food personalities have participated in the Charleston Food + Wine Festival over the years.

Some notable names include Anthony Bourdain, Sean Brock, Marcus Samuelsson, Carla Hall, and David Chang, among many others.

Charleston Fashion Week

Charleston Fashion Week is an annual event held in the city of Charleston, South Carolina that showcases emerging fashion designers, models, and local retailers.

The event was first launched in 2007 and has since become a premier fashion event in the Southeast, drawing fashion industry professionals and enthusiasts from around the world.

The event features runway shows, designer showcases, style competitions, and industry talks, and has helped to elevate the profile of Charleston's fashion industry.

Charleston Fashion Week is typically held in the spring and attracts both established and up-and-coming designers.

Charleston Fashion Week has had notable attendees and designers, such as Christian Siriano, Chris Benz, and Zac Posen, among others.

Celebrities such as Kelly Rowland and Andre Leon Talley have also attended the event.

Charleston Jazz Festival

The Charleston Jazz Festival is an annual event that celebrates jazz music and its roots in the Charleston community.

Founded in 2014, the festival brings together renowned jazz musicians from across the country to perform in historic venues throughout the city.

The festival is typically held in January and features a variety of concerts, workshops, and other events, including performances by local student jazz ensembles.

The festival is organized by Charleston Jazz, a non-profit organization dedicated to promoting jazz music and education in the Charleston area.

The Charleston Jazz Festival has featured many notable performers over the years, including Dianne Reeves, Arturo Sandoval, René Marie, Freddy Cole, and Gregory Porter.

The High Water Festival

The High Water Festival is an annual two-day music festival that takes place in North Charleston, South Carolina, just outside of Charleston.

The festival was founded in 2017 by local musicians Shovels & Rope, and features a lineup of well-known and up-and-coming musicians from various genres including indie, folk, Americana, and more.

In addition to the music, the festival also offers a variety of food and drink options from local vendors and artisans, as well as a "Low Tide Social" pre-party event and various other activities.

The festival takes place at Riverfront Park, which offers scenic views of the Cooper River and the surrounding marshlands.

Several famous musicians have performed at the High Water Festival, including Jason Isbell and the 400 Unit, Band of Horses, Wilco, Nathaniel Rateliff & The Night Sweats, and Margo Price.

The Charleston Bluegrass Festival

The Charleston Bluegrass Festival is an annual music festival that takes place in Charleston, South Carolina.

The festival features a lineup of bluegrass and folk musicians from across the country, as well as local acts.

The event includes performances, workshops, and other activities related to bluegrass music. It is known for its intimate atmosphere and beautiful setting on the grounds of the Middleton Place, a historic site located just outside of Charleston.

The festival was first held in 2017 and has quickly become a popular event for bluegrass fans in the area.

There have been several notable performers at the Charleston Bluegrass Festival, including the Steep Canyon Rangers, Po' Ramblin' Boys, and the Lonesome River Band.

However, it is not widely known for attracting big-name celebrities or performers. The festival focuses more on showcasing talented bluegrass musicians and promoting the genre.

The Lowcountry Cajun Festival

The Lowcountry Cajun Festival is an annual event that takes place in the town of James Island, just outside of Charleston, South Carolina.

It is a celebration of Cajun culture, featuring authentic Cajun and Creole food, music, and dance.

The festival includes a crawfish-eating contest, a children's area with inflatable rides and games, and an arts and crafts market.

Attendees can enjoy live music on two stages, with performances by local and regional bands, as well as nationally recognized artists.

The Lowcountry Cajun Festival is held every April and attracts thousands of visitors from around the region.

Southern Ground Music and Food Festival

The Southern Ground Music and Food Festival is an annual event held in Charleston, South Carolina.

The festival was founded by country music star Zac Brown in 2012 and features a variety of musical genres, including country, rock, and blues.

In addition to the music, the festival also showcases Southern cuisine, with a focus on farm-to-table and locally sourced ingredients.

The festival typically takes place over two days in the spring and has featured well-known musicians such as the Zac Brown Band, John Mayer, and Jason Mraz.

Willie Nelson, Gregg Allman, John Mayer, and Sheryl Crow also played at this festival the past.

Sweetgrass Cultural Arts Festival

The Sweetgrass Cultural Arts Festival is an annual event that takes place in Mount Pleasant, South Carolina, just outside of Charleston.

The festival celebrates the art of sweetgrass basket weaving, a tradition that has been passed down through generations of African Americans in the Lowcountry.

The festival features a variety of activities including live performances, arts and crafts vendors, and demonstrations of sweetgrass basket weaving.

It provides a platform for the preservation of the Gullah Geechee culture, which is deeply rooted in the Lowcountry region.

Gullah/Geechee Nation International Music & Movement Festival

The Gullah/Geechee Nation International Music & Movement Festival is an annual event held in Charleston, South Carolina, that celebrates the African American Gullah/Geechee culture.

The festival features live music, dance performances, storytelling, arts and crafts, and food vendors.

The festival aims to showcase the contributions of the Gullah/Geechee people to the Lowcountry region of South Carolina, as well as to promote cultural awareness and preservation.

The Gullah/Geechee Nation International Music & Movement Festival attracts visitors from all over the world and is a unique celebration of African American culture in the United States.

There have been several notable performers at the Gullah/Geechee Nation International Music & Movement Festival, including Grammy-nominated singer Marlena Smalls, the McIntosh County Shouters, and the Hallelujah Singers.

The focus of the festival is on celebrating and preserving the Gullah/Geechee culture and highlighting local artists and performers.

The Lowcountry of South Carolina is a hub of cultural activity and has a vibrant arts and entertainment scene.

From its rich history to its modern-day influences, the region offers something for everyone. The Spoleto Festival USA, Charleston Wine + Food Festival, Charleston Fashion Week, Charleston Gallery Association's Art Walk, Charleston Jazz Festival, High Water Festival, Charleston Bluegrass Festival, Lowcountry Cajun Festival, Southern Ground Music and Food Festival, and Sweetgrass Cultural Arts Festival are just a few of the many arts and entertainment events that take place in and around Charleston. Additionally, the area is home to numerous theaters, art galleries, museums, and other cultural institutions, ensuring that there is always something to see and do for both visitors and locals alike.

CONCLUSION

The Lowcountry of South Carolina is a unique and special place for many reasons. Its stunning natural beauty, with marshes, beaches, and tidal rivers, creates a picturesque coastal landscape. The mild and temperate climate allows for enjoyable outdoor activities throughout the year. But it's not just nature that makes the Lowcountry exceptional.

The area is steeped in history, with a rich cultural heritage that tells captivating stories. Charming towns like Charleston and Beaufort are home to beautiful architecture and fascinating historical landmarks. Exploring historic homes, wandering along cobblestone streets, and soaking in the rich history is a treat for history buffs and curious travelers alike. The Lowcountry is a place where the past comes alive.

And let's not forget the culinary delights of the Lowcountry. The abundance of fresh seafood and farm-to-table dining options make it a food lover's paradise. From iconic dishes like shrimp and grits to the indulgent flavors of she-crab soup, the Lowcountry's cuisine is a delightful blend of Southern traditions and coastal influences. The area boasts acclaimed restaurants that offer unforgettable dining experiences, where every bite tells a story.

For those seeking outdoor adventures, the Lowcountry has plenty to offer. Kayaking through the serene waterways, boating along the coast, casting a line for a day of fishing, or hiking the scenic trails—all these activities immerse you in the region's natural splendor. And golf enthusiasts will find their paradise with several world-renowned golf courses, where the breathtaking landscapes become the backdrop for a memorable game.

But what truly sets the Lowcountry apart is the warmth of its people and the genuine hospitality they offer. From the friendly locals to the welcoming communities, visitors are embraced with open arms. It's a place where strangers become friends, and every interaction leaves a lasting impression.

The Lowcountry of South Carolina is a destination that captivates with its natural beauty, rich history, delectable cuisine, and abundant recreational opportunities. It's a place where you can immerse yourself in the past, savor the flavors of the present, and create memories that will last a lifetime. So, whether you're seeking relaxation, adventure, or cultural enrichment, a vacation in the Lowcountry is sure to exceed your expectations and leave you longing to return.

Index

A

ACE Basin National Wildlife Refuge · 47
African American culture · 25, 26, 29, 111
African American heritage · 10, 12
African Americans · 31, 110
Aiken-Rhett House · 43
Alice Childress · 50
Alice Flagg · 10, 65
Alicia Rhett Mayberry. · 78
Alligators · 88
Alshon Jeffery · 57
American Revolution · 13, 33
Angel Oak · 24, 81, 89, 90
Angelina Grimké · 50
Anne Bonny · 63
Anne Rivers Siddons · 54
Army Wives · 90
Arthur Ravenel Jr · 21, 40, 55, 102
Arthur Ravenel Jr. Bridge · 21, 40, 102
Ashley River · 13, 18, 19, 20, 67, 85, 86, 87
Ashley River Historic District offers · 87
Atlantic Ocean · 14, 19, 20, 97, 98
Audubon South Carolina · 92
Automatic Gate · 39
Avenue of Oaks · 24

B

Bald eagles · 88
Baptist · 30
Barbecue · 72
barrier islands · 12, 14, 20, 26
Battery · 24, 36, 38, 61
Battery Carriage House Inn · 60
Battery Park · 36
beaches · 10, 14, 15, 17, 20, 22, 23, 25, 81, 82, 83, 84, 87, 88
Beaufort · 15, 16, 17, 18, 24, 25, 34, 36, 49, 53, 60, 67, 68, 71, 86, 94
Beaufort County · 15, 16
Beaufort Historic District · 24
Beaufort National Cemetery · 36, 67
Beaufort Water Festival · 94
Beaufort Waterfront Park · 86
Benne wafers · 75, 76
Berkeley County · 15
Beth Israel Cemetery · 67
Bethany Cemetery · 68
bike tour · 82
Bill Murray · 51
Bill Sharpe · 58
Bill Withers · 52
blackwater · 19
blackwater river · 19
Blue Crab · 72

Bluffton · 17, 18, 20
boating · 20, 22, 93
Bobcats · 88
boiled peanuts · 23
Bonneau Cemetery · 68
Boone Hall Plantation · 24
Bulls Bay Golf Club · 98

C

camping · 14, 84
Cape Romain National Wildlife Refuge · 92
Catawba Tribe · 28
Catholic · 38, 68
Charles Cotesworth Pinckney · 49
Charles Pinckney · 38
Charles Town · 13, 33
Charleston · 13, 15, 16, 17, 18, 19, 20, 21, 22, 24, 25, 26, 28, 29, 33, 34, 35, 36, 37, 38, 39, 40, 41, 49, 50, 51, 52, 53, 54, 55, 56, 57, 58, 59, 60, 61, 63, 67, 68, 69, 70, 72, 74, 76, 78, 80, 82, 83, 84, 86, 87, 88, 89, 90, 91, 92, 93, 94, 95, 96, 97, 98, 99, 100, 101, 102, 103, 104, 106, 107, 108, 109, 110, 111, 112
Charleston Battery · 19, 37, 38, 58, 100
Charleston Bluegrass Festival · 108, 112
Charleston Chews · 76
Charleston City Market · 24
Charleston County · 15
Charleston Earthquake · 34, 39
Charleston Earthquake Detector · 39
Charleston Fashion Week · 106
Charleston Harbor · 19, 20, 21, 22, 24, 35, 37, 38, 49, 85, 86, 93, 94, 95
Charleston Harbor Billfish Tournament · 96
Charleston Harbor Fest, · 93
Charleston Harbor Resort & Marina · 93, 94
Charleston Harbor Resort & Marina Billfish Tournament · 94
Charleston Hospital Strike · 34
Charleston In-Water Boat Show. · 93
Charleston Jazz Festival · 107, 112
Charleston Jazz Orchestra · 53
Charleston Lacrosse Club · 101
Charleston Maritime Festival · 94
Charleston Museum · 41
Charleston Outlaws · 101
Charleston Race Week · 93, 94
Charleston Receipts Cookbook · 39
Charleston Renaissance · 37
Charleston RiverDogs · 100
Charleston Rugby Club · 101
Charleston Sailing Week · 94
Charleston Sipper · 74
Charleston Symphony Orchestra · 52

Charleston Tennis Center · 99
Charleston Wine + Food Festival · 105
Charlton Singleton · 53
Cheaper by the Dozen · 55
Cheese straws · 77
Chief Justice · 51, 56
Christ Church Cemetery - · 68
Circular Congregational Church · 60
Citizenship Schools, · 49
Civil Rights Movement · 38
Civil War · 13, 21, 23, 28, 33, 35, 38, 49, 50, 56, 59, 60
Clams · 73
coast · 12, 13, 15, 16, 18, 20, 25, 55, 63, 64, 88
Coast Guard · 35
Coastal Discovery Museum · 47
coastal plain · 12, 14
Colleton County · 15
colonists · 13, 33
Combahee River · 19
Constitutional Convention · 49, 51
Cooper River · 17, 19, 21, 35, 40, 69, 87, 96, 102, 108
Cooper River Bridge Run · 102
counties · 15, 16
Crab Bank Seabird Sanctuary, · 21
crabs · 14, 71, 81
cuisine · 10, 12, 13, 22, 23, 30, 31, 32, 37, 39, 71, 72, 74, 75, 79, 80, 105, 110
Cypress Gardens · 85

D

Daniel Island Club · 100
Darius Rucker · 51, 52
Declaration of Independence · 50
Dock Street Theatre · 61
Dolphins · 88
Dorchester County · 16
downtown Charleston · 17, 24, 35, 69
Dr. Charles Shephard · 74
Dubose Heyward · 54
DuBose Heyward · 37, 50

E

E. Lee Spence · 55
Edisto Beach · 84, 95
Edisto Beach State Park · 95
Edisto Billfish Invitational · 97
Edisto Island · 14, 69, 80, 87, 97
Edisto Island National Scenic Byway · 87
Edisto River · 19
Edisto Tribe · 28
Eliza Limehouse · 52
Emily Geiger · 10, 62
English · 13, 31, 33
Episcopal · 30, 67
Esau Jenkins · 38
estuaries · 12, 14
Execution Dock · 63

F

Family Circle Tennis Center · 99
female pirate · 63
Firefly lighter · 39
Firefly Sweet Tea · 74
fishing · 19, 20, 21, 22, 25, 83, 84, 90, 91, 93, 94, 95, 96, 97
Flounder · 73
Folly Beach · 14, 81, 82, 83, 95
Folly River · 84
Fort Sumter · 21, 23, 33, 35
Fort Sumter National Monument · 46
Founding Father · 49, 50, 51
Francis Marion National Forest · 85, 92
Frank Gilbreth · 55
French Huguenots · 31
Fried Chicken · 72
Frogmore Stew · 71

G

Gadsden's Wharf · 44
George Washington · 43
German · 32, 68
ghost · 10, 59, 60, 61, 62, 63, 64, 65, 66, 69, 70
ghost animals · 69
Ghost Bridge · 60
ghost cat · 69, 70
ghost deer · 69
ghost dogs · 70
ghost horses · 69
Ghost of Drayton Hall · 70
ghostly boar · 69
ghostly figures · 59, 60, 61
Gian Carlo Menotti · 104
Gibbes Museum · 42
Gibbes Museum of Art · 69
Golden Age of Piracy · 37
golf · 17, 25, 37, 58, 83, 84, 97, 98
Goose Creek · 67
Gray Man · 10, 64
Greenlawn Cemetery · 68
Groundnut cake · 77
Grouper · 73
Gullah Geechee · 10, 12, 16, 22, 25, 26, 29, 30, 31, 37, 41, 45, 67, 79, 110
Gullah Geechee Cultural Heritage Corridor · 25
Gullah/Geechee Nation International Music & Movement Festival · 111

H

H.L. Hunley · 38
Hairy Houdini · 69
Harbour Town Golf Links · 97
Harbour Town Lighthouse · 24
HarbourFest · 94
Harleston Green · 37
Harriet Tubman · 49

haunted · 10, 59, 60, 61, 66
Heyward-Washington House · 43, 60
High Water Festival · 107, 108, 112
hiking · 14, 22, 25, 84, 89
Hilton Head Island · 14, 17, 18, 24, 66, 68, 94, 97, 102
Hilton Head Island Boat Show · 94
Hilton Head Island Concours d'Elegance · 101
historic homes · 10, 17, 23, 24
historic landmarks · 13, 16, 19, 23, 26, 82
Holy Cross Cemetery · 68
Hoppin' John · 71
Huguenot Torte · 78
Hunting Island State Park · 14, 25, 83, 84
Huntington Beach State Park · 65
hurricane · 34, 64
Hurricane Hugo · 34, 64
Hurricane of 1893 · 34
Hyman's Seafood · 80

I

I-26 · 18
I-95 · 18
International African American Museum · 44
Intracoastal Waterway · 20, 86
Irish · 32

Isle of Palms · 14, 64, 82, 83, 95, 98, 99
Italian · 32

J

Jake Shimabukuro · 53
James Island County Park · 83, 86
Jasper County · 16
Jenny Sanford · 56
Jewish · 30, 32, 38, 67
Jewish culture · 30
Joe Cunningham · 57
John Bennett · 54
John C. Calhoun · 50, 55
John Laurens · 51
John Rutledge · 51, 56
Johns Island County Park · 95
Joint Base Charleston · 21, 34
Joseph Bramah · 39
Joseph P. Riley Jr · 56, 100
Josephine Humphreys · 54
Julia Peterkin · 55
Junior League of Charleston · 39
Justus Angel · 89

K

kayaking · 19, 20, 21, 22, 82, 83, 84, 85, 86
Kiawah Island · 14, 20, 25, 83, 87, 96, 97, 98, 100

Kiawah Island Golf Resort · 83, 97, 100
Kiawah Island Parkway · 87
Kiawah River · 20, 85
King Charles II · 13
Kingstree · 18

L

Lady Baltimore cake · 78, 79
Lake Moultrie · 95
Lands End Road · 66
Laurel Hill Cemetery · 69
Lebanese · 32
Lemonade · 74
Lewis Timothy · 39
Lindsey Graham · 56
Live Oak Cemetery · 68
Lowcountry Cajun Festival · 109, 112
Lowcountry Kayak Anglers · 97
Lowcountry Redfish Cup · 97
Lowcountry Summer · 54

M

Mace Brown Museum of Natural History · 46
Magnolia Cemetery - · 67
Magnolia Plantation · 19, 23, 37, 59
Mahi-mahi · 73
marine biology · 22
Mark Bryan · 53

Marsh Tacky Horse · 39
marshes · 12, 14, 20, 22, 23, 26, 66, 69, 72, 81, 82, 83, 84, 85, 86, 87, 88, 89, 98
Martha Waight Angel · 89
Mary Alice Monroe · 54
Mary McLeod Bethune · 50
Matthew Roberts · 58
May River · 20
McClellanville · 61
Megadock Billfishing Tournament · 96
Middleton Place · 19, 108
Mills House Hotel · 60
Mint Julep · 74
Moncks Corner · 18, 85
Morris Island Lighthouse · 25
Mount Pleasant · 17, 35, 61, 68, 69, 84, 85, 87, 98, 99, 100, 102, 110
Mount Pleasant Waterfront Park · 87
Murrells Inlet · 65
museum homes · 43

N

Nathanael Greene · 62
Nathaniel Russell House · 25, 43
National Council of Negro Women · 50
Native American · 13, 28, 31, 41
Native American tribes · 13, 31

Naval Weapons Station Charleston · 35
North Charleston and Summerville Trail System · 87
Nowhere Else on Earth · 54
Nullification Crisis · 33

O

Oak Point Golf Course · 98
oceanography · 22
Okra Soup · 72
Old City Jail · 59
Old Exchange and Provost Dungeon · 60
Old Post Office Restaurant · 80
Old Sheldon Church Ruins · 61, 67
Old Village · 69
Oldest Liquor Store in the United States · 80
oyster · 20, 71, 85
Oyster Roast · 71
oysters · 14, 72

P

paddleboarding · 21, 82, 83, 84, 85, 86
Palmetto Beer · 74
Palmetto Trail · 87
Parris Island · 17, 34
Pat Conroy · 50, 53
Patriots Point · 35, 98, 100

Patriots Point Links · 98
Patriots Point Naval & Maritime Museum · 45
Peachtree Road · 54
PGA Tour · 58, 98
Phil Davison · 39
Piedmont · 14
Pinckney Drafting Table · 38
pirates · 63
Poogan's Porch Restaurant · 59
Porgy and Bess · 50, 54
Printing Press · 39
Prohibition · 37, 80
Protestant · 31, 38
Pulitzer Prize · 55

R

Rainbow Row · 24
Ranky Tanky · 52
Ravenel Bridge · 86, 87
Reconstruction Era · 33
red drum · 72
Red foxes · 88
Red Rice · 71
redfish · 83, 95, 96, 97
Redfish · 72
Red-tailed hawks · 89
Revolutionary War · 51, 60, 61, 62, 63
Rice Cultivation System · 38
Rich in Love · 54
River otters · 89

Riverfront Park · 86, 108
Robert B. Rhett · 56
Robert Barnwell Rhett · 50
Robert Porcher · 58
Robert Smalls · 49
Roy Barth Tennis Center · 100

S

sailing · 21, 93, 94
Santee Cooper Lakes · 95
Santee River · 20
Sarah Grimké · 50
SC-170 · 18
SC-61 · 18
Scarlet Sister Mary · 55
Scottish · 32
Sea turtles · 88
Seabrook Island Racquet Club · 100
Secession Convention · 33
Septima Clark · 38, 49
SEWE · 90, 91
Sewee Visitor and Environmental Education Center · 92
she-crab soup · 10, 23, 30
She-Crab Soup · 71
Sheepshead · 73
Shem Creek · 84, 96
Shem Creek Park · 96
Shovels & Rope · 107
shrimp · 10, 14, 30, 71, 72, 79, 80, 84

shrimp and grits · 10, 23, 30, 71, 79, 80
shrimp and grits, · 23, 30, 79, 80
Siege of Charleston · 33
sightseeing · 24, 36
Sir John Yeamans · 13, 33
Snee Farm Country Club · 100
South Carolina Aquarium · 92
South Carolina Department of Natural Resources · 92
South Carolina Ports Authority · 21
Southeastern Wildlife Exposition · 90, 91
Southern Charm · 52
Southern Ground Music and Food Festival · 109, 112
Spanish explorers · 28, 31
Spoleto Festival USA · 104, 105, 112
St. Andrew's Church Cemetery · 67
St. Helena Sound · 19, 20
St. Helena's Episcopal Church · 67
St. James Goose Creek Episcopal Church Cemetery · 67
St. James-Santee Episcopal Church · 61
St. Mary's Roman Catholic Cemetery · 68
Stephen Colbert · 52
Stephen Davis · 57
Stingray Shuffle · 40
Stono Ferry Golf Course · 98
Stono Rebellion · 33
Strom Thurmond · 56

Submarine · 38
Sue Monk Kidd · 54
Sullivan's Island · 82, 87
Summerville · 17, 18, 57, 68, 74, 75, 87
Sweet Tea · 73, 75
Sweet Tea Festival · 75
sweetgrass basket · 30, 37, 38, 110
Sweetgrass Cultural Arts Festival · 110, 112

T

Tavern At Rainbow Row · 80
Tea Punch · 74
The Beach House · 54
The Blind Tiger · 80
The Center for Birds of Prey · 47
The Citadel War Memorial · 36
The Fort Moultrie Loop · 87
The Great Santini · 50, 54
The House Next Door · 54
The Invention of Wings · 54
The Links at Wild Dunes · 98
The Palace Hotel · 80
The Patriot · 90
The Prince of Tides · 50, 54
The Secret Life of Bees · 54
Thomas Gibson · 52
Thomas Heyward Jr · 43
Thomas Heyward Jr. · 50, 60
Thomas Sumter · 62
tidal river · 19, 20

Tim Scott · 56
Troy Brown · 58

U

U.S. Congressman · 49
U.S. Constitution · 49
U.S. Navy · 35
Unitarian Church Cemetery · 61
United Soccer League · 100
US Constitution · 33
US-17 · 18
US-52 · 18
USS Clamagore · 45
USS Yorktown · 24, 36, 45, 61

V

Vertical-Lift Bridge · 40
Vice President · 50, 55
Volvo Car Open · 99

W

Waccamaw River · 19
Waccamaw Tribe · 19, 28
Wando River · 85, 87
Wando Riverfront Park · 86
Wappoo Cut Boat Landing · 95
water sports · 21, 94
West Ashley Greenway · 86
White-tailed deer · 88
Wild Dunes Resort · 83, 99

Wild turkeys · 88
wildlife · 10, 14, 19, 20, 21, 26, 81, 82, 84, 85, 86, 88, 89, 90, 91, 92, 93
William Gilmore Simms · 51, 54

Z

Zion Cemetery and Baynard Mausoleum - · 68
Zoe St. Amand · 59

ABOUT THE AUTHOR

Karen Lee lives in South Carolina with her Lowcountry born and raised husband. She is an avid backyard birder and information enthusiast.

ALSO AVAILABLE

Looking for trivia and facts on birds? Look no further! **Feathered Facts: A Trivia Book About Birds** covers everything from Anna's Hummingbird to Ziz.

Learn about bird habitats, nesting habits, and much more. With fascinating feathered facts, this book is perfect for bird enthusiasts of all levels. Whether you're a beginner or an experienced birdwatcher, you're sure to learn something new with every turn of the page.

Available on Kindle and in print on Amazon.

ALSO AVAILABLE

BIRD SEARCH USA - A Word Search Book for Bird Lovers

Birds are everywhere. Even when you can't see them, you can hear them. The United States enjoys a wide variety of wild birds. This book offers two large print word searches for each US state. These are the birds you would actually find in the state, with the official state bird indicated as well.

WORD NERD USA - United States of America - Themed Word Search Puzzles

This word search book contains puzzles for each state and US territory. There are also broader puzzles for American originated subjects such as food, television, movies, and animals. The large print book also features "mega puzzles" to extend the fun.

PUZZLED BY THE 80s

The 1980s were a time of massive economic and geopolitical changes. Yeah, we're not going to delve into any of that serious stuff. Instead, this book contains word searches, crosswords, cryptograms, and anagrams all themed around the pop culture of the 80s - movies, music, TV, fads, and more.

PUZZLED BY THE 70s

This book takes all the major pop culture milestones - all the cinematic trends, all the musical stylings, all the popular fads - and tosses them into a blender. Inside, you'll find dozens of word search puzzles, crossword puzzles, cryptograms, anagrams, kriss-kross puzzles, and even a few period-correct logic puzzles.

MOVIE QUOTE CRYPTOGRAMS

This book contains over 500 quotes from movies, ranging from the earliest of talkies to the most recent blockbusters. Some of the quotes are iconic and timeless, while others delve deeper into the movie - it won't be as easy as seeing the title and immediately guessing the quote!

ACADEMY AWARD WORD SEARCH PUZZLES

This book features 100 full size word search puzzles containing nominees for Best Picture, Best Director, Best Actor / Actress and Best Supporting Actor / Actress. The puzzles are broken down on a year-to-year basis so you can see who was up against whom and who took home the trophy. There are also puzzles based on most nominated writers, composers, and more!

Made in United States
Orlando, FL
15 August 2023